D1175387

THE CREED AS SYMBOL

THE CREED AS SYMBOL

Nicholas Ayo, C.S.C.

University of Notre Dame Press
Notre Dame, Indiana

Library of Congress Cataloging-in-Publication Data

Ayo, Nicholas.
    The creed as symbol.

    Bibliography: p.
    1. Apostles' Creed.   I. Title.
BT993.2.A94   1989   238'.11   88-40321
ISBN 0-268-00769-1

Manufactured in the United States of America

This book is dedicated to

Mary Catherine Rowland

who for more than twenty years
encouraged me to write this book

CONTENTS

ACKNOWLEDGMENTS

The author would like to thank the many people who made this work possible. I am grateful to my family, especially my ninety-four year-old mother, who still encourages her children, as well as to my religious family, the Congregation of Holy Cross. The Notre Dame Press and in particular John Ehmann and Carole Roos deserve special mention, along with the generous and unknown readers of my typescript. The Wilbur Foundation assisted me with a grant. Walter Nicgorski and Philip Sloan of the Program of Liberal Studies at the University of Notre Dame gave me every assistance. Juliette LaChapelle and Suzanne Lutz helped me as student assistants. Cheryl Reed, Nila Gerhold, Nancy Kegler, and Shirley Vogel in the Stenopool gave many hours to preparing the text. I would thank so many people who befriended me in this task: Elena Malits, C.S.C., Charles Sheedy, C.S.C., James Burtchaell, C.S.C., David Schlaver, C.S.C., David Burrell, C.S.C., Mary C. Rowland, Jay C. Harbeck, Catherine LaCugna, Genevieve Coulon Ayo, Alida Ann Macor, John Macor, Pamela DuPont, Brother Lee Barker, S.C., John Lyon, and several theology classes in the Program of Liberal Studies, especially the seniors in the Spring of 1984 and 1985.

INTRODUCTION

I

An author writes the book he or she is most able to write. That book awaits being born. Subsequently one writes an introduction to explain the book, and even to justify its inevitability in just the form it took. Parents are indeed proud of their children, and their children look like them, no matter their preference. I write about the catholic creed. It is a succinct formula of faith, and its phrases are beautiful and ancient. The creed lends itself easily to meditation; it yields further layers of meaning to investigation. The creed has been for centuries the vademecum for Christians, lifelong believers as well as catechumens. So short and so prayerful, the creed was committed to memory as the basic symbol and confession of faith. It was thus to be engraved upon the Christian's heart as well as held up before the mind.

My text is primarily the Apostles' Creed. It holds the kernel of the apostolic formulation of who Jesus Christ was believed to be. It sums up the Christian faith as it is found in the biblical scriptures. The origin of the Apostles' Creed centers around the liturgy of baptism, both the instructional preparation and the rite itself. The Nicene Creed, which amplifies and elaborates earlier baptismal creeds, adds to the simpler texts definitive conciliar formulations. We will take note of these emendations. The creed studied herein, however, is primarily Western. From the third century to the present it was formulated in Latin. We try not to lose sight of the Eastern creed and the Greek formulations at the origin of both creeds. Although the Apostles' Creed was not written by the apostles, it surely captures what they professed. Although what is popularly called the Nicene Creed was not altogether written at the Council of Nicaea, it captures the mind of that council and its attempt to preserve the mind of the scriptures by going outside of them for an articulation that would defend them.

One could approach the creed from the point of view of an historian, and try to trace its development in many places and over many

1

centuries. J. N. D. Kelly's *Early Christian Creeds* does just this in a masterful way.[1] Nonetheless, the record of how the creed developed contains gaps and conjectures. From time to time what had been concluded has subsequently been revised. Presumably the last word is still not spoken on the subject of the historical development of the creed.

One could approach the creed from an ecclesial point of view. How has the church used the creed? From its probable beginnings as an interrogatory creed used to elicit the catechumen's responses at baptism to its current place in the Sunday Eucharistic liturgy, the creed has played a role in the sacraments of the church. It can be found in liturgical texts for morning and evening prayers. It functions much like an ancient song, a canticle or psalm whose wording is venerable and untouchable now, no matter how the understanding and theological expression of doctrine might change over time.

One might study the creed specifically as catechesis. Until recent times the creed was the catechism of the church; it was the outline used for instruction of catechumens. Commentaries on the creed for those preparing for baptism abound. Rufinus of Aquileia, St. Ambrose, St. Augustine, St. Cyril of Jerusalem, Peter Abelard, St. Thomas Aquinas, and others have all written classic explanations of Christian doctrine in the form of commentaries on the creed. In the days when books were scarce and illiteracy was widespread, the distilled creed presented the catechumens with a text that could be memorized and pondered the rest of their lives. For centuries it was customary to hand the creed over to the catechumens at the beginning of their period of preparation, and then at baptism to require the public recitation of the creed by memory as the solemn profession of faith before the assembled Christian community. Augustine in his *Confessions* (VIII:6) narrates the moving scene when the well-known Roman pagan philosopher, Victorinus, embraced faith in Jesus Christ. The church was crowded with onlookers who came to see and hear Victorinus stand before them and profess the Christian creed aloud. Thus the creed was the confession of faith, the profession of hope, the protestation of a personal love. One bore witness to faith in the mystery of God who is beyond all formulations in this simple and public recitation of the rule or standard of faith that comprises the creed.

One could approach the creed as a way of teaching doctrine to those long since baptized. Karl Barth's *Dogmatics in Outline* seems to me a modern masterpiece of this genre. Jan Milic Lochman's recent book on the creed, *The Faith We Confess*, could serve as a fine example of how commentary on the creed as doctrinal exposition perdures. The creed can inspire sermons; Emil Brunner's *I Believe in the Living God* speaks to this purpose. Meditation on the creed remains an on-going task for all Christians. Ronald Knox's *The Creed in Slow Motion* and Paul Claudel's *I believe in God* might be noted in this genre.[2]

Nevertheless, it is not primarily as history, liturgy, catechesis, teaching, sermon, or prayerful meditation that I undertake to write of the creed. All of the above will enter into what is said about the creed, but the focus is slightly oblique to them all. I should like to write of the creed as *symbol*; it is the creed as sacred poem, as ancient psalm, as confessional litany, as extended metaphor, that I wish to address. The creed makes a poem of faith and theology; it is crafted carefully of exquisitely chosen words. Its form is economical: 75 words in the Latin of the Apostles' Creed, and 162 in the Latin of the Niceno-Constantinopolitan Creed (popularly called the Nicene Creed). Traditionally divided into twelve lines (in honor of the twelve apostles) and three stanzas (in honor of the Trinity), the Apostles' Creed deserves to be read as a poem, or symbol, with attention given to every word and every image.

Just like a sonnet, the creed could be divided into an octave that treats of the Father and Son, and a sestet that speaks of the Spirit's work of sanctification in the church and in the world. The sonnet form is thought to be an ideal size, long enough to develop an elaborate thought or image, and yet short enough to allow the reader to hold in mind the first lines while reading the last. I would argue that the creed functions in the same way. It is long enough to unfold the richness of faith, and short enough to be memorized as one magnificent sweep of words to ponder in one's heart.

This book is thus a study of creedal symbolization. The creed is a crystallization, a distillation, a concentration of the nutrient contents of faith. Into the creed are packed decades of reflection on Jesus Christ boiled down to a few sentences as the essence. Our task will be to disclose such a treasury. Like chemical analysis, literary analysis has limits. We can put a text through all kinds of empirical tests and still not know what the document means. Analysis of a literary sort will tell much, but it will not tell everything. Therefore, literary analysis will be combined with theological study and reflection. We will undertake some literary criticism of an ancient poem, as well as a theological criticism of a wisdom text. The emphasis is balanced between the literary and the theological, the form and the content, the body and the soul, the medium and the message. The division of these aspects as a methodology will be done with the recognition that in reality they cannot be separated. Moreover, the starting principle remains that the medium is the message, at least in part. I am interested in the literary aspects of the theology, and the theological aspects of the literature. Thus this book will focus on the creed as symbol, ancient and venerable, the "symbol of faith," as it was called for centuries.

My work is not located on the frontier of scholarship. What is original will stem more from my own metaphors and illustrations that seek to revivify overly familiar materials. Yet, this book uses the results of the scholarship of others, and perhaps contributes here and there a bit of its own. Some history of the creed serves as explanatory. The general tenor of biblical scholarship in the last few decades is presupposed. A willingness to consider Latin and Greek words is asked.

In the following pages the reader will be given enough history, Bible, and language to make his or her own way. But, the appeal will be to literature as well as to theology, to spirituality as well as to doctrine, to inspiration as well as to information, to devotion as well as to critical analysis of the creed. The book may thus seem a curious blend of passages of subjectivity and then objectivity, of impressionistic overview and yet data analysis. Heart and head are not divided, but they may well seem confused. The author's problem was this. How much scholarship is helpful for the reader, not too little nor too much? How much commentary of my own is worthwhile, neither too much to distract the reader nor too little to leave the creed unsung?

II

The creed has been called the symbol of the faith (symbolum fidei), and there is considerable dispute over the meaning of the word. How did early Christians understand the symbol, and why was this word chosen to describe it? Its application to the creed appears first in the West, and only later in the East, and that despite the fact that the roots of the word are Greek. Rufinus of Aquileia, who gave us a popular account of the apostles as authors of the creed and also valuable information about the Old Roman Creed, thought the word had two meanings: "Symbol in Greek can mean both sign and collation, that is what brings together many into one."[3] Both sign or indicator, and collation or collection were the meanings Rufinus assigned. Fol-

lowing the legend of the group authorship by the apostles, the interpretation of *symbolum* as collation of articles seems to have been early
favored. Thus we read: "Symbol in Greek means collation in Latin,"
a saying attributed to St. Ambrose.[4] When Thomas Aquinas came to
write his commentary on the Apostles' Creed, it was called "Collationes Credo in Deum" (Sermon-conferences on I Believe in God). He
himself thought that the word meant a gathering of separate articles:
"It is from its being a collection of propositions of faith that the symbol (in Greek, symballein) takes its name" (ST I–II, q.1, a.9). Augustine, however, followed the other line of descent and held that the
symbol was a special kind of sign or indicator. Thus he writes: "Symbol is so called from a certain similarity, given a word translation,
because merchants among themselves make a symbol as the pact of
faith that sustains their society."[5] Symbol here would seem to suggest a contract among business men, an ancient equivalent of a check,
a bond of some sort, a coin in its original sense of a token that could
be redeemed for something else.

J. N. D. Kelly explores the meaning of *symbolum* in some depth
in both his book *Early Christian Creeds* and in his translation and
notes on Rufinus' *Commentary on the Apostles' Creed*.[6] He concludes
that Rufinus started the account of a dual meaning of the word *symbolum*, and that the line of descent from *collatio* or collation is in
error. Accordingly, Rufinus is confusing the Greek, *symbolon* (sign)
with another and similar Greek word, *symbole* (collation). Kelly believes that sign or indicator is the "basic sense" of the Latin term
symbolum.

Several theories about *symbolum* as sign have been put forth.
We have already seen how Augustine used the sign value to talk of
contract or pact. This meaning easily led to seeing the creed as the
verbal covenant, contract, or bond of the baptismal commitment.
Other commentators saw the symbols and signs of the mystery religions as the exemplification of the proper usage of *symbolum*. Thus
the creed would be some kind of arcane knowledge, much like in our
own time the emblem of the carpenter's tools of the Freemasons. What
Kelly prefers, however, is that the *symbolum* be traced back to the
interrogatory creed, when three questions were asked of the catechumen: Do you believe in the Father, and in the Son, and in the Holy
Spirit? With each question there was a response, followed by an im-
mersion. That threefold question-response-immersion was a symbol
of the Trinity, and thus the creed was symbol of faith. The declarative
creed we now use grew out of these short baptismal questions as an
elaboration of them. To this day the creed is divided clearly into three

parts. Kelly writes: "The grand discovery to which our lengthy discussion has led is that the classical name for baptismal creeds was itself in origin bound up in the most intimate way with the primitive structure of the baptismal rite."[7]

The creed no longer functions readily as symbol of the threefold interrogations that in turn symbolized the blessed life of the Trinity, but it may still function as a poetic symbol even in its declarative form of twelve articles. The purpose of the present study is to note such symbolization in the creed. The creed as *symbolum* is the creed as symbol or poem. It is a sign which stands for something else; it is metaphor where words describe another reality. The creed is symbol in the literary sense of the word, and it points to the mystery of God, symbolized in the poetical and literary arrangement of these words and these sentences, of these creedal parts and divisions. The Latin word *tessera* has been suggested to explain the *symbolum*. The word *tessera* stands for a pass—ID cards carried by students, for example, that identify them and allow them to enter a performance without charge, or as a password among soldiers. Thus the symbol of faith functions as a *tessera* among Christians, a passport to the Kingdom of God, a *token* or spiritual sign of the identity of faith in Jesus Christ entrusted to the Christian.

In the Old Testament story, Tamar pressed upon Judah to leave with her his signet ring as a sign of his intent to pay her. Judah leaves his seal. In contemporary language, we might speak of surrendering a credit card. These signs or tokens stand for our substance; they stand for us. So, the creed was the credit card of the church; it was handed over to the catechumen to treasure and to guard. At their baptism they were to render back the credit card, now as the pledge of their own self-giving and spending of themselves upon the Lord. "Set me as a seal upon your heart"[8] is a way that we speak of spousal commitment. The recitation of the creed by heart and in heart was a betrothal ceremony, and the *symbolum fidei* functioned as the verbal gold wedding band. Such a token is a sign of one's faith and love. The ring seeks to express by its composition something precious, incorruptible, bright, and beautiful. Both the creed and the ring are signs that are the message; both are quasi-sacramental signs that bring about the message, that is, efficacious signs. It was in the very recitation of the *symbolum* by heart at baptism that the catechumen not only gave intellectual account of his or her faith, but actually entered into the sacrament or mystery of faith by an act of faith that was embodied in the recitation of that ancient symbol.

III

How the creed is arranged in its parts, in the divisions of each article, in the placement of the articles, and in the selection of the precise words, makes up a fascinating study, which we will undertake in the subsequent pages. The medium is surely a part of the message, and the analysis of such an accomplished poem pays precise attention to the relationship of parts to parts and parts to whole. We will look at each article individually and in depth, and we will look at whole sections of the creed for their value as a constellation of symbols. We will look at the entire creed as an icon and as a complex symbol-metaphor of the mystery of God.

My overall purpose in this book is to talk about these many levels of symbolic meaning that the few words of the Apostles' Creed might reveal. Ambrose writes: "Now is the time and day that we should hand over the symbol, which symbol is a spiritual seal, the meditation of our heart, and the almost always constant guard, surely the treasure in our breast."[9] Augustine concludes his "De Fide et Symbolo" with these words: "This is the faith, which in a few words contained in the symbol is given to new Christians. These few words are known to the faithful, so that by believing they might submit to God, submitting rightly they might live, rightly living they might have a clean heart, and clean of heart they might understand what they believe."[10]

One might ask, then who is this book written for? It is not aimed at scholars primarily, although I would hope they might find a synthesis of the results of scholarship presented in an attractive way. The book is written for the non-specialist or generalist, which is what I would call myself. I am addressing any college-educated person, either younger and in a classroom setting, or older and in a continuing education environment. The book might serve well as a supplement to a college text, as a parish renewal source book, or as a fundamental work for cathecumens of any Christian persuasion. I would hope to do what Henri de Lubac writes of his own enlightening book on the creed:

> Rather, we have tried to make it a sort of introduction to catechesis, addressed to all those who, either in preparing candidates for baptism or in teaching children or in day-by-day preaching to the Christian people, are entrusted with this most beautiful of all roles: handing on the faith received from the Apostles, al-

ways and infinitely fruitful even as it was when they themselves received it from Jesus Christ.[11]

This book runs the risk of proving too scholarly for popular readership, and too superficial for scholarly rank. It may prove too theological to satisfy the literary critic, and too literary to attract the theologian. One foot is planted in an academic investigation, the other foot in the task of the rhetorician to make the material speak. The reader will judge if the following pages do what I intended. This is a book of interdisciplinary concerns, and it will have to make sail under that flag for whatever harbor will welcome it.

The creed may not appear to be an adequate summary of the Christian faith for some readers. What is absent from both the Apostles' and the Nicene creed calls attention to itself. There is no mention of ethical commandments. Worship would seem to be given precedence over ethics; being over doing; what we are as children of God and brother and sister of Jesus rather than how we behave. No doubt action follows being, and the creed does not denigrate righteous living in any way. It remains, however, a confession of the deeds of God and the work of grace, more than an account of human initiative and virtues. There is also no explicit mention of the Eucharist in the creed, although the Nicene Creed to this day remains part of the Eucharistic liturgy, both in the East and in the West.

The creed enjoys universal acceptance and respect among all Christian groups. While the Apostles' Creed remains less a part of the tradition of the East, it contains the essence of all the most highly regarded apostolic creeds, both East and West, of the early centuries of Christianity. The Apostles' Creed is used in the West for the sacrament of baptism, and specifically in masses for children. The Niceno-Constantinopolitan Creed adds to that core symbol of faith only the phrases that elaborate the Lordship of Jesus Christ, and those that address the divinity of the Holy Spirit. Today the creed is used in the liturgy, both Protestant and Catholic. Thus, the creed makes for an ecumenical foothold, common and sacred ground on which all Christians can stand proudly and solidly, and from which they can pray together.[12]

A BRIEF HISTORY OF THE CREED

I

The rudiments of a creed can be found in the sacred scriptures of any religion. Creeds make explicit what may appear in the sacred text implicitly. Creeds distill the essentials, whereas commentaries more leisurely elaborate and illustrate matters. Thomas Aquinas says that "the articles of faith stand in the same relation to the doctrine of faith as self-evident principles to a teaching based on natural reason" (II–II, q.1, a.7). The creeds are thus attempts to summarize what is the basic and essential content of the scriptures, to isolate the few central and indispensable principles that prevail throughout the much longer anthology of writings collected over centuries and in which there is repetition, various viewpoints, and multiple expressions of the same mystery of God. Ambrose reminds the catechumens about to be baptized that the creed is a breviary of faith: "The holy apostles, gathered together as one, composed a breviary of faith, so that we might comprehend briefly the scope of our entire faith."[1]

Beginnings of the creed antedate the writing of the Gospels and Letters of the New Testament. Elements of the creed are among the most ancient formulations of Christian belief of which we know. Christians gave some account of their belief to themselves and to others for four or five decades before the canonical writings we now have began to emerge. In that time the apostolic teaching was phrased in certain ways, ways we cannot directly know but can surmise from the redaction of the scriptures themselves. The Acts of the Apostles record the baptism of the Ethiopian eunuch, for example, and the creed of faith he recites is brief and to the point: "I believe that Jesus Christ is the Son of God" (8:37). "Jesus is Lord" remains a succinct creed, and if one must be limited to three words, it is hard to imagine a more comprehensive statement of the Christian mystery of God's salvation. Longer and more narrative creedal expressions can also be found. Paul writes: "For I delivered to you as of first importance what I also received, that Christ died for our sins in accordance with the scriptures, that he was buried, that he was raised on the third day in accordance

9

with the scriptures and that he appeared to Cephas, then to the twelve" (1 Cor. 15:3–5). The sermon of Peter after Pentecost recapitulates the creed very substantially (Acts 2:22–37).

The Old Testament yields creedal crystallizations in many places. For a parallel core declaration to "Jesus is Lord," the Old Testament says: "The Lord, he is God; the Lord, he is God." (1 Kings 18:39). A narrative version of the creed can also readily be found, for example:

> A wandering Aramean was my father; and he went down into Egypt and sojourned there, few in number; and there he became a nation, great, mighty, and populous. And the Egyptians treated us harshly, and afflicted us, and laid upon us hard bondage. Then we cried to the Lord the God of our fathers, and the Lord heard our voice, and saw our affliction, our toil, and our oppression; and the Lord brought us out of Egypt with a mighty hand and an out-stretched arm, with great terror, with signs and wonders; and he brought us into this place and gave us this land, a land flowing with milk and honey. (Deut. 26:5–9)

Gradually as the apostolic teaching spread and was further developed, the need for a formulation that could be used as the basis for instruction for baptism, and for the liturgical profession of faith in the sacrament of baptism itself, was also recognized. Creedal formulations were somewhat lengthened and carefully crafted with words well chosen to distill the essence of the Christian faith. The need to teach and preach stimulated theological reflection on the creed. The need to defend the faith before critics and to confess one's allegiance before persecutors made short and slogan-like affirmations of faith very useful. These phrases were concentrated food, cryptic and full of packed meaning. The unpacking of the creed became the kind of theological endeavor that occupied the catechumenate and led to the development of many Patristic commentaries on the symbol of faith as a resumé or prècis of the entire teaching of the faith. Thus Nicetas of Remesiana could write to his catechumens: "The words of the creed are few—but all mysteries are in them. Selected from the whole of Scripture and put together for the sake of brevity, they are like precious gems making a single crown. Thus, all the faithful have sufficient knowledge of salvation, even though many are unable, or too busy with their worldly affairs, to read the Scriptures."[2]

Many of the Fathers of the church have left us commentaries. Cyril of Jerusalem wrote his *Catechetical Lectures.* One could add Rufinus of Aquileia "Commentary on the Apostles' Creed," Nicetas of Remesiana "De Symbolo," Ambrose "In Symbolum Apostolurum

Tractatus," and Augustine "De Fide et Symbolo," as well as his "Enchiridion." In the Middle Ages, the commentaries on the creed continued. One might note Abelard "Exposito Symboli (quod dicitur Apostolorum)" and Aquinas in his sermon-conferences explicating the creed, "Collationes Credo in Deum." Apparently the tradition of systematic theology as commentary on the traditional *Sentences* grew out of the earlier practice of commenting upon the *articles of faith* encapsulated in the creeds.

The scriptures fixed the apostolic teaching in its overall content. However, the creeds, which in their basic elements claim descent from the apostolic tradition, continued to evolve. Creeds were the scriptures in development, and they continued to be refined for several centuries. Just as there was a great variety of local Christian churches throughout Asia Minor, Africa, and the West, so there was a bouquet of creeds. Like the liturgical rites themselves, local color and language and custom helped to shape these creeds. Christians were to memorize the creed, to meditate upon it in their prayer, and to live it in their life as a disciple of Christ, rather than write it down somewhere and then proceed to forget all about it. Many of the instructions given to catechumens at the time of their baptism make much of this Christian practice of rendering the creed by memory. Instructions in the faith were given personally and orally to the catechumen by the local church into which he or she was to be incorporated by baptism. Local liturgies and local creeds were various and the text often in flux. What is remarkable is not that there are many creeds, but that the differences are so slight, and that agreement about the essentials remains so widespread.

II

In the West, the less formal liturgical creed continued to develop. Originally it was found in a series of questions asked of the catechumen at the time of the reception of the sacrament. Usually the trinitarian threefold division was employed, following the dominical command at the end of Matthew's Gospel to preach to all nations "baptizing them in the name of the Father, Son, and Holy Spirit" (28: 19). Today we do much the same with the interrogations at the Easter Vigil. Gradually a declarative creed that could be elaborated, memorized, and recited developed. Called the *symbolum apostolorum*, or Apostle's Creed, it claimed its origin in the teaching of the apostles. Attempts were even made, particularly by Rufinus and Priminius, to attribute each article of the creed to a separate apostle, who composed it while the apostles were still in Jerusalem together after Pentecost.

By the fourth century, when Christianity became a recognized religion of the Roman empire, we begin to have fuller documentation of the many creeds. Marcellus of Ancyra, Rufinus of Aquileia, and Nicetas of Remesiana give us even then the basic Western creed.[3] The earlier Roman Creed, sometimes called the Old Roman Creed, is lost to us in its exact form, just as the exact sayings of Jesus are probably lost to us. What texts we have are later creeds (fourth century and afterwards) solidly based on the earlier Roman Creed, which was itself based on the apostolic teaching. J. N. D. Kelly calls the *Romanum* (the Old Roman Creed) the "primitive kerygma of the apostolic age."[4] The Roman Creed gave birth to many different creeds, and was in turn influenced by other creeds. Several late additions make the Apostles' Creed more fulsome than the Old Roman Creed (see Appendix). Their inclusion in what became the "established text" dates between the fourth and eighth centuries, even though the doctrines were themselves much older. Their introduction into the creed was gradual, with some instances earlier than others. Nicetas of Remesiana gives us almost the "established text" of the Apostles' Creed (c. 400), but the first example of the "established text" of the Apostles' Creed in exactly the version we know it today would seem to come from Priminius (c. 725).[5]

The baptismal liturgy in the West originally employed versions of the Roman Creed, then used the Nicene Creed for several centuries, and finally settled upon a popular descendant of the Roman Creed, which is the Apostles' Creed that we recite today. J. N. D. Kelly calls the "established text" of the Apostles' Creed "simply a provincial elaboration of the Old Roman Creed."[6] In other words, several articles of faith were added to the *Romanum* from the liturgies and practice of churches outside of Rome, especially Gallic churches. "The descent into hell" and the "communion of saints" are but two of these late-established additions, even though the doctrine they formulate goes back to the ancient apostolic teaching.

The Apostles' Creed is more concise than the Nicene Creed. Moreover, the Apostles' Creed is a biblical creed that professes the Christ event in terms of the narrative theology of the Bible. One might wish to compare the Apostles' Creed with the narrative theology of the Synoptic Gospels, and the Nicene Creed with the more systematic theology of a St. Paul or a St. John. In one of his sermons, Augustine could say to the catechumens prior to their reciting by heart the creed at the time of their baptism: "These words which you hear are scattered through the scriptures, but from them they have been gathered and edited, lest the memory of slower persons struggle, and so that every person can say them and can hold on to what he or she believes."[7] The Nicene Creed placed into the creed of faith a non-scriptural term, "homoousion," not found in the Bible. This and similar elaborations of the creed give justification in principle to a systematic theology that would further develop a biblical theology.[8]

III

Cyril of Jerusalem, the Nicene (325) and Constantinople (381) Councils, as well as several provincial councils in the East, give us the basic text of the eastern creed. The so-called Nicene Creed was essentially fixed by the end of the fourth century. Although the Nicene Creed had roots in the baptismal creeds of many of the ancient churches of Asia Minor, the eastern creed was a conciliar creed, a declarative creed, a symbol of the Fathers (symbolum patrum). After the Constantinian peace of the Edict of Milan, several hundred Fathers of the church, mostly eastern, gathered in Nicaea (325) at the Emperor's invitation to draw up a document of creedal unity. Political as well as religious disputes abounded. The creedal additions of the Council of Nicaea consist largely of the expansion of the Christological second part of the creed, where the Lordship of Jesus Christ is confessed. "Consubstantial (homoousion) with the Father" became the touchstone of orthodox belief, although it remained possible to misread even this carefully crafted anti-Arian discrimination for many years.

The established text of the Niceno-Constantinopolitan Creed that we use today was put forth at the Council of Constantinople (381) where some 150 Fathers of the East gathered about fifty years after the Council of Nicaea. Because of the polemical disputes about the nature of the Holy Spirit, additions were made to the third part of the creed that touched upon the equality of the Holy Spirit with the Father and the Son. The Niceno-Constantinopolitan Creed ratified the work of the Council of Nicaea and was in turn ratified by the whole church. The Council of Ephesus (431) would discourage the further development of yet new creeds, and the Council of Chalcedon (451) officially approved the Nicene and Niceno-Constantinopolitan creeds as the creeds of Christendom, both East and West. What is still popularly called the "Nicene Creed" enjoys to this day broad support among Christians and remains a unifying document for East and West, and for Protestant and Catholic. The rift between East and West over the insertion of the "filioque" clause in a Western version of the Niceno-Constantinopolitan Creed dates from the Middle Ages and shows as much a political dispute as a religious one.

The Council of Trent (session in 1546) affirmed the Niceno-Constantinopolitan Creed as the official creed of the church: "We determine that the symbol of faith, used by the holy Roman church, as that principle, in which everyone, who professes faith in Christ, comes together necessarily, and that firm and unique foundation, against which the gates of hell never will prevail, must be expressed in so many words, which in all the churches are read."[9] During the Reformation, doctrinal confessions and creeds, such as the Augsburg Confession, abounded. To this day many elaborations of the creed continue to appear, for example, Paul VI's "Credo of the People of God" (1968). Translations of the creed sometimes raise issues of doctrinal meaning. Nevertheless, since Trent there have not been any further substantive developments of the creed in the Roman Catholic church.

IV

Despite the idiosyncrasy of so much of liturgical practice and the history of creedal formulation, it is surprising how many creeds agree upon the basic outline of the doctrine of faith. Clearly the creeds followed the "rule of faith" and a genuine and ancient apostolic tradition, and that was their least common denominator. Nonetheless, the question before us now as students of the Apostles' Creed remains this: How shall we articulate the creed? What are the articles of faith? If we do a study of the comparative anatomy of the body of the creed, where are the joints? Which bones belong in what classification? The creed remains an organic body of truths that are interrelated like the members of a body, and yet the tibia is not the fibula. How many articles of faith are there and what are their proper names?

Common opinion would hold there are twelve articles in the Apostles' Creed. The popular legend has long been that the Apostles' Creed represents in some way the twelve apostles and their teaching. It is Rufinus of Aquileia who early notes the tradition (or perhaps more exactly, the legend) that each of the apostles contributed one article of the creed. According to his commentary, after the descent of the Holy Spirit at Pentecost, and prior to the dispersal of the apostles throughout the world to preach the risen Christ, they composed together a formulation of their faith. Each of them was invited to contribute one article to affirm in unity and consensus the essence of their belief in Jesus of Nazareth.

Rufinus does not assign each article of the creed to a particular apostolic author. Priminius, however, who gives us the "established text" several centuries later, does attribute each of the articles of the creed to a particular apostle as author of it. Priminius' listing does not completely agree in attribution with other authors, such as pseudo-Augustine, who gives a quite different account.[10] Nevertheless, when biographical lists are compared, the order of the names of the apostles remains more or less consistent, and seems to conform roughly to the order of being chosen apostles by Jesus himself as recounted in the Synoptic Gospels, where agreement is also more or less consistent. Even the Council of Trent, long after the legend of apostolic authorship was in decline, continued to number twelve articles to the creed, but without specific attribution to any of the twelve apostles.

The usual order of attribution is as follows. Peter is always given article one, "I believe in God." Matthias, who took Judas' place and was last chosen, is almost always given article twelve. James and John, the close associates of Jesus, who are brothers and the sons of Zebedee, usually are given articles two and three. Then Andrew, brother of Simon Peter, is given article four. This order follows Mark (3:16–19) and Acts (1:13). In all the Synoptic Gospels, it is Philip who is next chosen, and usually he is given the next article, which is usually reckoned to be the "descent into hell." On all lists I have seen Thomas is given the next article, dealing with the resurrection, even though such an attribution puts him out of the order of apostolic selection in all the Gospels, although not in Acts nor in the eucharistic canon of the *Missale Romanum*. No doubt John's account of the "doubting Thomas" made it irresistible to attribute the resurrection article of faith to Thomas the Apostle. The Gospels list the order of selection after Philip to be: Bartholomew, and then Matthew and Thomas, (vice versa in Matthew), then James the lesser (son of Alphaeus). Finally, Thaddeus (Jude or Judas not Iscariot) is followed by Simon the Zealot (vice versa in Luke), with Judas Iscariot always listed as the last. The attribution to the articles of the creed follows roughly this order. Peter, James and John, and Andrew always head the list, though Andrew is sometimes second, following Matthew (10:2–4), Luke (6:14–16), and the *Missale Romanum*. Philip is given the "descent into hell"; Thomas is given the resurrection article. Simon, Jude, and Matthias can be counted on at the end of the list. The remainder fill in, now this way, now that.

Given the legend of the twelve apostles composing the creed article by article, and given the tradition of twelve articles that survives to this day, the question should now be raised how shall we compose these articles? There has not been unanimity about the divisions of the Apostles' Creed. I find there are twenty clauses in the Apostles' Creed. These are as follows:

1. I believe in God
2. Father almighty
3. Creator of heaven and earth
4. And in Jesus Christ
5. His only Son our Lord
6. Conceived of the Holy Spirit
7. Born of the Virgin Mary
8. Suffered under Pontius Pilate, was crucified
9. Was dead, was buried.
10. Descended into hell
11. On the third day he rose again
12. He ascended into heaven
13. Sits at the right hand
14. He will come to judge the living and the dead
15. I believe in the Holy Spirit
16. The holy catholic church
17. The communion of saints
18. The forgiveness of sins
19. The resurrection of the body
20. (And) life everlasting.

These twenty clauses must be reduced to twelve articles, if the tradition is to be maintained. Eight clauses must be yoked. Almost everyone agrees that 1 and 2 and 3 should go together, and that the pairing of 4 and 5, 6 and 7, and 8 and 9 seems reasonable. There is hardly an example that does not yoke 12 and 13. Thus only two more clauses must be combined. No one puts forth "the communion of saints," which is a late-established addition, to stand alone as a separate article. However, there remains endless controversy over whether it belongs with "holy church" or with "the forgiveness of sins." The issue thus reduces itself to finding one more clause to yoke, and the candidates are either "the descent into hell" or "life everlasting." Both of these are not found in the Old Roman Creed, and as late-established additions they have been positioned loosely in the creed.

The problem could be solved in one of two ways: (1) the "descent into hell" is yoked, either by joining it with "suffered, was crucified, was dead, and was buried, *and descended into hell,*" or by combining it with the following article. Thus "*he descended into hell;* the third day he rose again from the dead." (2) The other possibility is to yoke "life everlasting" with "the resurrection of the body." That has been done in many creeds, and the frequent presence of the conjunction "and" lends some argument to so doing. Thus, "the resurrection of the body and life everlasting" would become the last article of the creed. If the "descent" is yoked, then the "resurrection of the body" remains the eleventh article of the creed, and "life everlasting" the twelfth.

My own solution to the articulation of the creed follows Priminius primarily. I offer my own arguments for this arrangement, lacking any from Priminius. The "communion of saints" is yoked with "forgiveness of sins." The controversy is extensive, and the only argument I want to put forth here is that there is a parallel with the Niceno-Constantinopolitan Creed's formulation: "one baptism for the forgiveness of sins." Thus the sacraments of the church are put together and given emphasis. Furthermore, "resurrection of the body" is yoked with "and life everlasting." Both phrases are given in the Nicene Creed, and they are found together with the conjunction. Moreover, "resurrection of the body" and "life everlasting" appear to be twin ideas, such as space and time. They are not the same thing, but they are related closely and easily combined in one article.

Along with Priminius and a few others I am arguing for making the "descent into hell" a separate article of the Apostles' Creed. If it is combined with "suffered . . . buried," which the numbering in Trent does, it sounds like the "descent" only means Jesus was truly dead and buried. If it is combined with "third day he rose again," as most modern commentators do, it steals the thunder of the resurrection article, and it appears to point only to the anticipation of resurrection that is found in the harrowing-of-hell tradition. I should like the "descent" to keep both meanings and belong to both articles on either side of it. The simplest way to have it both ways would seem to be to place it as a separate article, sandwiched between the passion and the resurrection. The early commentators, who assign the twelve apostles by name, generally give the "descent" entirely to some one of them, customarily Philip and sometimes Thomas. An argument against giving the "descent" separate article status could possibly be made from its absence in the Eastern creeds. And yet, we find the doctrine of the "descent" well established in the Eastern Fathers. The very influential catechetical instructions of Cyril of Jerusalem talk of the "descent" in several places.

The arrangement of the articles of faith does provide an immediate practical problem. How shall the material of a commentary be presented in article by article divisions? But beyond that, does the division of the articles of the creed suggest different understandings of the given article? If the "descent into hell" is placed with the "passion" does it necessarily have a different meaning, or at least emphasis, compared to being yoked with the "resurrection" article? Does the "communion of saints" take on one meaning when joined with the "church" article, and another when combined with "forgiveness of sins"? Is "life eternal" more germane with "resurrection of the body" when these two are joined with the conjunction? These are fair questions.

Let us try to answer them. It could be that where an article is positioned already reflects how that article was understood. It could also be that where an article is placed contributed to how the article has become understood. In short, the positioning could be consequence or it could be cause. It is also possible that it makes no difference how it is placed, even if the positioning was once done deliberately. Texts are read often without adverting to format, which may even be a matter only of editorial thoughtlessness. My own view is this. We cannot show why the positioning happened as it did, and in fact, there is no one incontrovertible orthodox arrangement of the text. The Vatican standardized the text of the creed largely to facilitate prayer in common, but such a disciplinary decree does not pretend to be historical validation for the exact wording and composition of articles. The evidence for a historical solution of how exactly to divide the articles of faith remains indecisive, and what I put forth is an arrangement or articulation with pedagogic advantages, and as much historical support as an opposite division. How the articles are set up in any commentary will accomplish this much; it will call attention to where the emphasis is being placed, and make one reading easier to support than another. I would claim little more than this.

*Meditations upon the
Apostles' Creed*

PROLOGUE

Occasionally one hears believing Christians say that they find no difficulty believing the articles of the creed, except for one or two, about which they hold some reservations. The difficult-to-believe articles of faith might even be marginal ones, such as the virgin birth or the descent into hell. My perspective will differ. I hold that all of the articles of faith are difficult to believe, for all of them attempt to formulate in yet another way the ineffable mystery of God. Each article of the creed far exceeds our human reason, and each presents us with an adamantine facet of the infinite God in the incomprehensibility of God's wisdom.

Some explanations of the articles of the creed more softly accent this mystery of God, and others more insistently underline the ineffable depth of God. In these latter explanations the paradox of belief is accentuated at every turn. Let us offer such a comparison, briefly at the beginning of each article. I shall call the less accented reading of the creed the "immediate insight," and the more accented account the "further insight."

Also, as an epilogue, let us summarize each article of the creed under the rubric of the mystery of the One and the Many that we will see as a constant thread in our article by article elaboration of the Apostles' Creed. The One and the Many comprehends the mystery of God. It presents the mystery of the seemingly contradictory coexistence of the infinite and the finite, the uncreated and the created world, the One and the Many.

However, the One, the infinite Being, is more readily spoken of with the metaphor, Lord. God is the One; therefore, God is the Lord of all. "Lord," captures the Old Testament history for those with that background of faith. "Lord" can serve also as *sovereign* for those of a more humanistic background. When the metaphor is applied to God, it creates an analogy. On the one hand, God is Lord as we understand "lord" given whatever our background, and on the other hand, God's Lordship surpasses all that the word could possibly contain.

In speaking of the lordship of God, the creed also speaks to our human condition. What is said of God is not just information for the

21

curious. God's reality shapes our own, illuminates it, and lends it ultimate worth and meaning. Our summations of each article of the creed will follow this twofold division: what is said of God and what follows for humankind.

ARTICLE I

To TURN TO THE first article: "I believe in God, the Father almighty, creator of heaven and earth." The immediate insight sees God as one participant among many in the world. Indeed, God is the one most powerful and most wise. Indeed, God is bigger than any other influence in the world, yet God remains one among many.

The further insight sees God as precisely not one more participant among many in the world. God is within and under and around and below and above all the participants in the world. God is more than big. Not measurable by any category, God does not fall into any genus. God is unique. God dwells everywhere; God sustains everything. God knows all and provides all that happens. Thus God is not one, however great, among many. God is the One. God is the mystery of the infinite One, so great that God could somehow even put outside such immensity the Many of creation. Yet never for an instant does God not sustain the being of all things and guide the doing of all events. Whether over naturally determined things or humanly free persons, God reigns as Lord of the world. God is sovereign over all that exists. Should God not sustain all anew each moment, the world would fail to be at all. God made all; God makes all; God enters all. Yet creation is not God, and the human freedom that God conceives and moves from the inside remains genuine freedom. Thus, God is incomprehensible as well.

Credo

The Latin "credo" means "I believe." To believe is a primary human capacity. Belief cannot be reduced to some prior, more simple, and easier to understand life experience which might explain it. As with the primary colors, no appeal to some more fundamental color can be made. Reason is one color; faith is another basic and irreducible color. Faith need not clash with reason, but neither can it be reduced to reason or be overturned by it, nor brought about in the believer by reason alone. As human events are related to history, so faith is related to theology. One can find fault with the explanations of history and those of theology; one cannot undo the events nor replace genuine belief in those who believe. In the last analysis, God is not made in the image of human reason; it is human reality and experience that are made in the image of God. God is primary; all else is derivative. Belief cannot be reduced to a species of some other experience. To believe is a given and hardly understood capacity of human nature.

To believe also involves to trust. The belief that is of grace and leads to faith's new commitment to life calls forth trust. Faith gives rise to trust, which is hope, and then and thus to love. Faith remains not solely in dogma propositions or creedal statements, but in the God to whom and from whom the words lead. God may be imaged in words, but God is never captured by words. Trust in God gives soul to the body of faith about God. Cardinal Newman speaks about a "real assent" to the claims of faith that otherwise generate but a "notional assent."[1] It is for such a reason that St. Thomas Aquinas could call faith the "beginning of heaven" which "unites the soul to its spouse" even while it dwells on this earth.[2] Even human faith, which is the solidarity of human beings in the reliability of what we attest to each other, exhibits this conjunction of belief and trust. I believe that my parents were my parents and that such are the facts. I believe these facts because I trust my parents' testimony to be trustworthy. Thus I believe in my parents and trust them as the source of my being and the defender of my welfare. So also, we believe *in* God, both that there is a God and that this God is somehow for us. We believe thus in God who calls us to knowledge and to love, who illumines our minds and enkindles our hearts as well. We believe in the God who would have us believe not only of God but most of all in God.

To believe also involves to do. We cry the Gospel with our lives and not only with our creeds. Truth is something we must do. Action follows being. Actions speak louder than words. Should we follow someone throughout a day, we would discover what they believe by how they behave. One might suspect in many instances that those who seek the true, defend the good, cherish the beautiful, do indeed believe in God. Even if they have not heard the word, or even if they set the word aside because what they have been told of God has been presented by imperfect believers who often mislead by poor theological argument or scandalize by poor ethical living, nonetheless such people believe. The good man or woman believes in the Good. All truth is from the Holy Spirit. To hope amidst the human predicament presupposes hope in God in order to persevere at all.

Some people never talk of God in a thematic way; they eschew religion. Their life, however, declares the mystery of God just as the heavens declare the glory of God. These are hidden and anonymous faithful. And conversely, some people who tell of God, but do not show forth God in their lives may not believe in the way that saves, and in the manner that puts their life in trust into the hands of God. To believe in the love of God entails to begin to love, and vice versa. "If anyone says, 'I love God,' but hates his brother, he is a liar; for whoever does not love a brother whom he has seen cannot love God whom he has not seen" (1 John 4:20).[3] God is not fooled by words that are not winged words, which do not go to the heart of the matter. Don't just tell me, show me. Ideally we confess our faith in words and proclaim it in deeds. Living faith gives birth to good works, or faith is dead, according to St. James in his Epistle. Works alone cannot make us just, but made just we work. Having known the love of God, we live out the love of God. That is why the creed contains no ethical commands or statements. It is enough to say "I believe in." Rightly understood, to believe in word is also to love in deed.

The word "credo" itself might possibly come from Sanskrit roots which implicate two Latin words *cor dare*, which could be translated "to give one's heart." The word "believe" is derived from the German *geliefe*, which in turn is related to *geliebe* (love).[4] To believe is thus to be-love, just as to betroth is to be-truth one's promises. One of the Old English versions of the creed begins with "Hi true in God."[5] I put my truth in God; I trust in God. These various meanings are related in etymology as well as in theology. That kind of trusting and loving faith is closer to a marriage covenant than to the conclusion of a ratiocination. One commentator compares belief to a marriage proposal. "Once the proposal has been made, an answer must be given. Once it has been spoken and heard, neither the lover's 'Will you marry me?' nor Jesus' 'Will you follow me?' can be evaded.[6] As Gregory Vlastos has written, 'There are a thousand ways of saying no; one way of saying yes; and no way of saying anything else.'"[7]

Thus to believe is personal; faith is from God as person who loves and to God as person to be loved. To believe is a gift; it is not the product of argumentation, as helpful as that effort may be. Only in part do we trust because of the historical evidence. Ultimately trust remains a leap beyond the givens. Such belief calls for an unconditional bond whatever the future may hold. Faith boasts of a gratuitous grace and a loving invitation, and not of the fruit of human effort or prudent calculation. God is trustworthy, because to the extent that we risk leaning on God, God gives support. There is no demonstrating the support that would touch our lives, if we do not in our faith lean upon the very person of God to whom we are truly united in the faith that remains ultimately God's self-giving to us. To initiate a conversation, which conservation the Bible records, is already to befriend the listener, and that even prior to any specific content of the words.

When we look at God from the vantage point of our own independent reason, which assesses the evidence for belief, we stand in an illusion. There remains no independent viewpoint from which and outside of the infinite God we could evaluate the claims of God. We are already within the bounds of an all-embracing God when we begin to think about the validity of our thoughts about this same God, although to us perhaps an unknown God then and there. To believe seems like a circle, because one must first believe in order to believe. We experience our initiative in turning to the question of God, but in reality our turning is the response to a question put to us by God in our very existence. From such a circle the only remedy is to acknowledge the mystery of existence. Because we are not our own source of being, we have no absolutely independent and completely-outside-of-God starting point. To this mystery of the Sovereign God, this mystery of the One and the Many, this almighty God who is more me than I am myself, we all can finally only cling.

Deum

The Latin "Deum" means "God." To believe in God is not to believe in one more person in the room, or even one more being in the world. God is not one among many. God is the mystery of the infinite One Being from whom issues all the many beings and without whom, even for an instant, none of them could exist. Yet, no one of them is God. God is not another being in the universe, albeit the biggest one. Rather, God remains in, under, above, about, and around everything in the world, and yet these many things are not God. Nor are created beings any part of God, even though they can never escape God. God is the mystery of the One and the Many, where what is mysterious is that anything besides God should ever exist. If God is infinite, if God is affirmed in a manner worthy of an infinite God, if God is everything, how can something be anything? Yet we are not God and we exist, permeated by the being of God who creates and sustains us. Thus the existence of God is more obvious and necessary than my own. That God exists should seem patent; the existence of the world is the question. God is not the genus and we the species. God is beyond genus; He is sui generis; She is unique. Wherever we may go, God has forestalled us and arrives ahead of us. If we call upon God, it is not our idea but our response to God's first calling upon us to call upon God. God is ahead of us at every turn; we think we walk, but we are also carried in God's arms. God holds the whole world in God's hands. She foresees all; He provides everything. As creation is related to being, so providence is to doing. Thus there is nowhere to flee, no place to stand on one's own without God. The Psalmist well knew this sovereignty of God:

> Whither shall I go from thy Spirit?
> Or whither shall I flee from thy presence?
> If I ascend to heaven, thou art there!
> If I make my bed in Sheol, thou art there!
> If I take the wings of the morning and dwell in the uttermost
>   parts of the sea, even there thy hand shall lead me, and thy
>   right hand shall hold me.
> If I say "Let only darkness cover me, and the light about me
>   be night," even the darkness is not dark to thee, the night
>   is bright as the day; for darkness is as light with thee.
>   (Ps. 139:7–12)

God is the plenum; all being participates in God. That "participation" is a mystery, and the existence of the creature far less intelligible than the being of the creator in all its fullness. The many colors of the rainbow are the refractions of the fullness of white light. That light we never see itself. "In thy light do we see light" (Ps. 36:9). "In him we live and move and have our being" (Acts 17:28). God is the "field"; we are the objects contained in its borders. God is the infinitely rich white page; we are the ink scratches barely distinguishable in the dazzling light. Without that white field we are darkness and nothingness. Similarly, God is the fullness of silence; we are the voice that breaks the pregnant silence without whose fullness we would be absolute non-sense. Thus God is assumed just as the air we breathe and the gravity that grasps us. God ever remains our first resource, despite the popular tendency of prayer of petition to call upon God only as a last resource when our own efforts have proved impotent.

To believe in God is to believe in the infinite, yet not as the negation of all limitations we can imagine, as if God were only the negative absence of any definition, a boundless potency as it were. To believe in the infinite is to believe in positive Being sustaining always and everywhere all being. It is to believe in the absolute fullness of God's Being, infinite *ipsum esse subsistens*,[8] absolute active sovereignty. God sustains all being; God does all things. This is to say more than that God can do everything. Everything that happens in its most profound and ultimate explanation remains God's doing. God is thus not found in history as one force among many; history is found in God. Such was the biblical assumption of faith in God. Only sin, which is the absence of being, escapes God's doing. Even human freedom remains God's doing, who created freedom itself and maintains its integrity while moving it from within its very being. Even sin does not escape God's providence, for God's sovereignty prevails even over the non-being of sin. God writes straight with crooked lines. Just as God's being was sovereign over the non-being or "nothing" of creation, so even more mysteriously we find God creating good even out of the evil that has nothing of God's being. Such is the sovereignty of God. Neither being nor non-being fails God.

If there were no sovereign and infinite God, then we would receive our existence, not as a gift but as a factual and unexplained event. We call mere facts a "given," but genuine givens depend upon a giver. Actually, even "facts" call upon the existence of a factor. Without God, there can be no meaning. If there were no God, it would ultimately be our limited mind that validates what is true, that gives any intelligibility to the "sound and the fury." If there were no God, it would finally be our will that decides what is good, that establishes its own freedom beyond good and evil. Thus we are then finally sovereign, lords of our own being, and there can be no God beyond humankind. Alone, absurd, and autonomous we are necessarily skeptical. How ever do we exist and why?

Conversely, to believe in God is to discover the truth and not to fabricate it, and to find people as family rather than resent them as "other." To believe in God is to receive one's life as a gift from a "whom," to whom one can give thanks "always and everywhere." To believe in God is to be quickened into life by another, and to discover in God an unconditional and gratuitous love. Without God I am on my own and this world is all I have got. With God my life is a gift and the fear of deadend death is overcome by a love of the infinite God that affirms I am too good ever to cease to be.

God (Deum) in article one of the creed is not primarily the God of the philosophers or just a generic word for God. The word points back to YHWH, the unnamed and ineffable name of God in the Old Testament, and it points forward to the Father, Son, and Spirit in the mystery of the Trinity in the New Testament. In the creed there remains only one God, Immanuel, God-with-us. The creed holds in tension the understanding of God in both Testaments, Old and New, and it presents a seemingly generic word to hold forth the God who is anything but generic. God remains unique. The few words that follow the word "God" (Deum) in article one comprise one long qualifying and constitutive adjective that imperfectly tries to give a proper name to God, insofar as human language might dare to do so.

The Nicene Creed adds the word "one" God. What the older Roman Creed assumed as understood, the conciliar creed spells out. Controversies in the fourth century concerning the Father and the Son had raised the issue of whether a derivative and diminished divinity was implied by claiming the Son was true God along with the Father. In reality, the creed is all of one piece. Although Jesus Christ does not appear until article two in the creed, one need not conclude that Christianity is a second step after Theism. Jesus Christ remains the fullness of the revelation of the Father, and there is only *one* God. Not everything can be said at once; not everything about God was revealed at once. The God of the Old Testament, and the God of the philosophers for that matter, should not be considered necessarily in opposition to the God of the New Testament, who is Jesus Christ Our Lord. Rather the truth about God is built on the principle of analogy. Creation says something about God that is true; revelation in the Old Testament says even more; and Jesus who spoke of Abba says all that could be said in words.

Patrem Omnipotentem

The Latin "patrem omnipotentem" means "father almighty." Because we do not believe in a generic God, we proclaim our belief in the creed to be belief in the "father" who is God. More exactly, we believe in "God-the-father-almighty." We do not believe in just God, a generalized God who happens to be father. We believe in fathergod, or godfather, who is pattern and paradigm of all fatherhood under heaven. God is not made in the patriarchal image of human fathers; fathers (and mothers) are made in the image of God. We believe in the fertile source-God, the expansive origin-God, the infinite sovereign-God, the fatheralmightygod. The Bible speaks of the fatherhood of God as the fountain of life, both the life of the world and the life of Our Lord Jesus Christ. The Father Almighty is *Yahweh Sabaoth*, the Lord of Hosts, the *Kyrios Pantocrator*, the Lord of History of the Old Testament, who includes the prehistory of the Genesis accounts of "in the beginning." The religions of the world, insofar as they yearn to know a God beyond this world, all seek to know the one infinite God.

Father (almighty) was construed in the creed by the early Christians not only with the lower case that spoke of the Lord of History of the Old Testament, but also with the upper case which spoke of the Abba-Father of Our Lord Jesus Christ. Father cannot be father without issue. The fathergod is related to the world in a correlative way in the mystery of creation; the Father is related to the Son in a correlative way in the mystery of the Trinity. Father Almighty has overtones of the great deeds of God in Jewish salvation history, as well as the Father Almighty about whom Jesus said, "The Father is greater than I" (John 14:28), even though "The Father and I are one" (John 10:30). Thus the creed does have implications of the Trinity even in its beginnings. The first article is the first part of a tripartite creed that confesses not a generic God who became human, but that the only begotten Son of the Father became a man. God gave not impersonal godly life to us, but God gave God's intimate life to us by the gift of the Son who reveals to us the Father. In this sense, God-the-Father-Almighty declares a secret proper name, like YHWH, unknown to any mind unless the Father choose to reveal it. God-Father remains not only the source of all being, but also and finally, God-Father is the Abba-Father of Jesus of Nazareth, who is the only begotten Son.

If God "Father" declares the proper hidden name of God, perhaps "Father" as proper name pointing to the God who surpasses all names would sound less sexually preferential. God has no body, nor sexual reference, and hence transcends both male and female. Though masculine metaphor about God predominates in the Bible, feminine metaphor is not absent or unimportant. When Isaiah says, "Can a woman forget her sucking child, that she should have no compassion on the Son of her womb" (Is. 49:15), the maternal nature of God is valued.

God is the fullness of being, and hence the fullness of motherhood and fatherhood. Finally, the ineffable God transcends all words.

To the extent "Father" is not understood as a proper name but as an adjective and metaphor, one might ask why "father" to describe God. Part of the answer lies in the understanding of human procreation when the Bible was written. An undeveloped biology credited the male with a greater role in reproduction than the female. His seed contained the life force, and her womb was as the nurturing earth to the seed sown. Moreover, an undeveloped sociology gave power and education to males without equal opportunity for females. Given the nature of power in primitive societies and the demands of child bearing, perhaps it could not have been much different. Prejudice is also likely. Yet there remain some partial truths about God hidden in the masculine imagery of the Bible. Creation from nothing, rather than from preexistent matter, does seem a doctrine more embodied in the metaphor of a father's role in the creation of new life. The contribution of the father seems so inconsequential, so momentary and detached. Furthermore, to please a father remains a clear choice for son or daughter, who may choose to obey or not. They may conclude that their father is dispensable enough to allow them to claim their independence and freedom. To displease a mother is more than a child can contemplate; upon her one is obviously dependent for food and the wherewithal for life. A child is related to its mother much as the human race is related to fertile ground. We speak of mother earth, and the ancient world knew the fascination of fertility cults, religious deference and sacrifice offered to the feminine power of life. Thus perhaps something of the independence of creation stands forth in the image of God the Father, creating from nothing a world that is not an extension of God's self, as a child tied to its mother might seem in popular imagination. The father-image is more detached and transcendent; the mother-image more attached and imminent. Both speak of God when properly understood. However, the exchange of God and human being might more easily be seen as independent and transcendent in the relationship of father and child, than the dependence, however good and necessary, between mother and child. Nonetheless, I do not wish to deny any maternal goodness and virtue in God, but only to speak of the metaphor "father" in a positive way. I believe in the motherhood of God and the sisterhood of man. The richness of the womanly metaphors for God still are to be appropriated, though their day may indeed have dawned. Both mother and father imply a child in order to be parent. Consequently, the world is home to us and God is parent who brings us into being and gives us our inheritance.

"Father Almighty" renders the Latin for "Patrem Omnipotentem." Both "almighty" and "omnipotent" connote power in reserve, rather than power at work; they speak more of boundless potency than of act. The Greek translation in the *Septuagint*, which antedated the Latin *Vulgate* translation of the Bible, renders the Hebrew *Yahweh Sabaoth* as *Kyrios Pantocrator*. Panto-crator says more than potentially all-powerful; the Greek emphasizes God as all-sovereign, all-ruling, all-doing in the world. Just as auto-crat means self-ruler, so panto-crat might be translated as all-ruler. Pantocrator was the complete Lord of History. God was pantocrator and not just panto-dynamos, which would be the Greek equivalent of omni-potens, or all-mighty. One of the Old English creeds translates "omnipotentem" as *aelwealdend*, rather than by the more customary word, *ealmihtig*, for almighty.[9] God is all-wealing; God is Lord of the Commonweal. The wealth, the wellness and welfare of all events flows from this *aewealdend* king of kings. Thus God is infinite power (potestas) and not just infinite potency (potentia). In short, God is sovereign and not just almighty. To that, "Father Almighty" adds that God's power is fatherful, and God's fatherhood is powerful. God is a power that gives life, a potent father, and one most able to defend his children. God's love is power (creation); God's power is love (providence). *Father* is Lord of being, and *Almighty* is Lord of doing. God Father is almighty creator; God almighty is fatherly provider. One commentator writes: "Almightiness denotes the power of God to fulfill all his fatherly purposes and creativeness denotes the fatherliness of all the purposes that God fulfills."[10]

How we pray may tell us how we believe. *Lex orandi, lex credendi*.[11] To believe in God-Father-Almighty, the sovereign and infinite God, is to believe not only in the fullness of creation but also in the fullness of providence. This is not the Deistic God, who stands by the history of the world, removed and detached, or hand-wringing along with the rest of us. Such a God remains impotent in the face of human freedom cast loose upon the history of the world. Believers, however, pray to the God who intervenes in the affairs of humankind; they pray to the God who makes the sun rise and the birds sing. They pray to the Lord of History for events big like peace in the world, and for events small like a sunny day for a picnic. Believers pray for the macro-world of "Thy Kingdom come" as well as the micro-world of "Give us this day our daily bread." They know whom to ask and what to ask; they ask for everything, taking nothing that happens for granted. Nothing remains too large to be impossible to God, and nothing too small to be disregarded.

Believers know whom to thank for events that turn out well,

and whom to thank for events that try their faith. Believers ask "do not lead us into temptation" and "do not put us to the test." They seek not events that try their faith in the wisdom and goodness of such a sovereign God. This world has not been cast free like an errant space laboratory beyond control. Therefore, believers know they must give thanks "always and everywhere." Their God foresees all, forestalls all, controls from within and gently all. Sovereign within our human freedom which God moves by God's grace precisely as our freedom, God remains pervasive throughout the very creation and supreme from within it. God's grace is efficacious, yet never destructive of the nature of true freedom. Sovereign and superior overall, God numbers the very hairs of our head. Each of us is known by name. Nowhere is God's sovereignty more evident than in God's triumph over sin and death. In the work of grace, in the reconciliation of brother and sister, and the conversions of our hearts to love, God remains the Almighty Creator bringing good, not just out of nothing, but bringing good out of the negative handicap that is sin and evil. God writes straight with crooked lines. Even sin serves the Almighty. If God can create out of nothing, God can create anew out of death. Creative of all power, God is not just power made enormously big. God remains beyond power. The Almighty is not one power among many powers, although the largest one. God is sovereign over power itself, which is God's creature. Thus, God may be weak as well as strong. God dwells in the natal crib as well as in the earthquake. Exalted or made humble flesh, the Almighty God remains supreme and sovereign, without equal or comparison.

Creatorem Coeli et Terrae

The Latin "creatorem" may be translated "creator." To the extent that Father Almighty was read as Abba-Father of Our Lord Jesus Christ, and less as *Kyrios Pantocrator*, Lord of History, the addition of the redundant "creator" along with "father," and "heaven and earth" along with "almighty" reinforced the original pre-Christian meaning of the creed. The Old Roman Creed, which preceded the "accepted text" established since the seventh or eighth century, did not include this synonymous repetition. The more ancient Christian creed assumed, of course, that the father of the universe was none other than the sovereign creator from nothingness whom both Hebrews and Christians have acknowledged. Just as creation "in the beginning" was not found in an early stage in the Old Testament literature, but rather reveals a later and more mature understanding of God, so the creator in the creed is a late-established addition that brings out the implications of God-Father. In both instances we speak of the God of the mystery of existence, the God of the One and the Many, whose very being is necessary, because our own contingent and seemingly impossible finite reality has no adequate cause within to exist at all.

The Latin "coeli et terrae" means "heaven and earth," or celestial reality and terrestrial. Heaven and earth stand for all that is above and below, spiritual and physical, eternal and temporal, night and day, everything from "a" to "z," as well as whatever might yet be discovered in the universe. The Nicene Creed changes this phrase to "things visible and invisible," things seen and unseen, the world of things and matter as well as the world of intelligibility and spirit. Humankind is the creature of matter and spirit, body and soul, suspended between earth and heaven and spanning them both. Humankind is the summation and apex of the creation of heaven and earth. This creedal phrase implicitly rejects any dualism that might judge the spirit from heaven above to be a good creation, and the earth below to be an inferior or evil product. All that God made, God saw and of it said: "It was good."

EPILOGUE

Lord of Being

In the first article, God is Lord of being (creation), and Lord of doing (providence). God is father (being) and almighty (doing). God is Lord of creation, Lord of the beginning, Lord of life, and Lord of everything. God is acknowledged in the first article as the infinite One, the sovereign One.

What is said about us follows. We are thus the Many; we are finite, contingent, and unnecessary. Our very existence remains the great mystery. How can anything truly exist alongside of the infinite, and yet not outside of the infinite? Our existence is precarious from a metaphysical viewpoint; we are never the cause of our own being, not even the ultimate cause of our own doing.

ARTICLE II

To TURN TO THE second article: "And in Jesus Christ, his only Son, our Lord." The immediate insight sees Jesus Christ as God made human. He comes from God to save us from the broken world of original sin, that disaster of Adam and Eve that set the world on a course of failure unless rescued by a savior. Jesus is the wonderful redeeming presence of God. Indeed, he is God with us, God made human.

The further insight sees Jesus as the infinite One become the finite Many. The Many is thereby taken up into the One from which it originally sprang. Jesus Christ is infinite mystery. The contradiction of the limitless infinite God and the finite creation is reconciled and united in his body. God remains God, and man remains man. Moreover, in Jesus Christ we have more than God made human. It is the Son of God who became human. It is the only Son of the Father, one in being, who takes our flesh to himself. Here we have more than a creator's gift, more than a rescue for a sinking world. Here we have the mystery of God giving, not just gifts, but self-gift. God gives the only Son; God bestows God's intimate self. In giving the Son, once and for all, the Father has given us personally everything. God can give no more. Nor can God ever take the gift of self back. The flesh of Jesus cannot be undone. No matter what we do, even if we crucify him, the gift of God's only Son remains irrevocable. Indeed we are more than saved. The world has been lovingly taken up into the intimate and infinite life of the Trinity.

Et in Jesum

The Latin "et in Jesum" means "and in Jesus." The name of Jesus comes from two roots: the short form of the word for the mysterious and unnamed God of Moses and the people of Israel, the YAH of alleluia, and the root word for "save." *Yehoshua* signifies YAH saves; in English we say "Joshua." "Jesus" is a shortened form of Joshua. The name suggests "he who saves," the God who saves, the savior. To all observation, however, Jesus of Nazareth evokes the ordinary inhabitant of a particular town in Galilee during the Roman occupation. The last several years of this man's pedestrian life were marked by an extraordinary prophetic and ministerial vocation. He was a Jewish itinerant preacher, full of power and signs, a man of remarkable teaching and powerful deeds, a holy man of unsurpassed integrity, who was "anointed" by the Spirit of God to proclaim the coming of the Kingdom of God among the people of Israel.

Because Jesus of Nazareth is so rooted in history, known to us by what he said and did, we come to love him just as we do a figure from the ancient past whose biography is not scientifically documented. His memory is preserved by the people who loved him as he walked this earth and who wished to keep the memory of him alive. The second article of the creed begins with the mention of the proper name of a man, a human being like us, a man called Jesus. The more we know of him and contemplate the accounts of his life, the more we might hope to be drawn to admire and love him as a fellow.

This love for Jesus, the man from Nazareth, does not yet represent the love of God. It remains a human love for a human being, rooted as are all human loves in the particularity of a singular voice and the limitations of a specific place and time. Yet, we need to remind ourselves that the love of another human being does not compete with the love of God. God is the infinite one, from whom and in whom all the many beings of creation exist. We do not love several people and God a one more on top of them all, bigger and more important. God is the infinite love, from whom and in whom all the many loves of human beings exist.

What then happens when we love a particular person, such as Jesus of Nazareth? In the willingness of our hearts to cling to a particular love, we discover, beyond what any of the human antecedents could validate, an invitation to enter into the love of God as the horizon within whose embrace we are enabled to love human beings and God at the same time. In short, we come to love Jesus and to love God at one and the same time, not only because Jesus is Son of God, but also because the mystery of creation in the history of time and space always involves the infinite God. Such a love teases our will to embrace the Creator whom we cannot see in the embrace of the creature whom we can see. The figure of Dante's Beatrice that leads human love to divine love has captured Christian imagination.[1] Human loves hold out the promise of union with God that cannot be consummated in this life. Human loves are sacramental; they point to God and coax the heart.

Jesus is not only a particular person to us, a unique identity never to be repeated, finite and precisely differentiated as all once only and never repeated historical realities must be, but Jesus is also the only begotten Son, who calls his father, Abba. It is not God who became human; it is not a generic God who entered history in some more or less involving way. The only Son of the Father leapt down from heaven in the still of the night. The unique bond of Father and Son is reflected in the unique bond of Abba and Jesus of Nazareth. The scandal of the historicity of the enfleshment of God in Jesus of Nazareth, what Kierkegaard called "the scandal of particularity," has its parallel in the scandal of the unique mystery of the Father and Son.[2] We know the mind of the Creator because we have seen the heart of the Father and Son. Here is not just necessary goodness, here is serendipitous revelation of infinite freedom. St. Paul comments eloquently on the mystery of Jesus:

> Have among yourselves the same attitude that is also yours in Christ Jesus, Who, though he was in the form of God, did not regard equality with God something to be grasped. Rather, he emptied himself, taking the form of a slave, coming in human likeness; and found human in appearance, he humbled himself, becoming obedient to death, even death on a cross. Because of this, God greatly exalted him and bestowed on him the name that is above every name, that at the name of Jesus every knee should bend, of those in heaven and on earth and under the earth, and every tongue confess that Jesus Christ is Lord, to the glory of God the Father. (Phil. 2:5–11)

The creed inserts an easily overlooked conjunction, "and," in the beginning of article two. It has been read disjunctively as a separation of the Father who is not the Son, from the Son who is not the Father. Thus one believes in God the Father plus Jesus Christ the only Son.

This conjunction has also been read more conjunctively as the unification of Father *and* Son. Thus the Father gives everything of his
infinite being to the Son who returns all to his Father. Thus we believe Father and Son are one; the relationship itself remains the only
distinction within the one true God.

Christum

The Latin "Christum" means "Christ." Jesus is the Christ, that
is, the *christos,* which is the Greek *Septuagint* translation of the Hebrew word, "Messiah," which signifies the Lord's *anointed* one. The
Latin word for anointing is *unctus,* from which we derive the naming
of the sacrament of Extreme Unction. The church anoints with
Chrism, that is, with ointment. Christ, therefore, means the anointed
one of God. The kings, priests, and prophets of Israel were chosen by
God through the agency of his holy prophets who embodied the spirit
of God. The sacramental gesture that corresponded to this divine elec-
tion was the laying on of hands and the anointing of the head with
oil. Grace was thus rubbed into the chosen one, whose body was to
be the vehicle of God's will on earth.

Jesus, who was the Christ, represented the truly anointed one,
the awaited king, the desire of the nations, the prophet-priest-king
Messiah promised and foreshadowed in the *gesta Dei*[3] throughout the
salvation history of Israel. All that history was prologue and preparation for the coming of the unique son of God, the Messiah of Israel
foretold by the prophets. In his baptism (and other epiphanies such
as the "transfiguration") Jesus is declared the beloved son by a voice
from heaven, and he is anointed by the Spirit from above in the form
of a dove that rests upon him. Here was God's chosen one, the culmination of the ages of awaiting, the embodiment of the reign of God that
was here and now in the midst of men and women, and even within
them. Pilate nails these words to the top of the cross: "Jesus the Nazo-
rean, the King of the Jews" (John 19:19). Although meant as a sardonic
title, those words contained a hidden prophetic proclamation. God
enthroned his anointed king on Calvary hill; he was lifted up above
all kings, king of kings for all eternity.

Later usage would run together "Jesus the Christ" into an equivalent proper name, Jesus Christ. The title Christ Jesus, or Messiah Jesus, would be equivalent to a title that has become part of a famous
person's name. So, we speak of Cardinal Newman, Kaiser Wilhelm,
and Pope Pius, as if we were giving the first and last names. Simi-

larly, Christians speak of Jesus Christ, or following the practice of St. Paul, Christ Jesus. How sacred and beautiful these words that announce the hidden name of the Son of God on human lips. Unlike the tetragrammaton YHWH, which no one could utter, the name of Jesus Christ we call upon every day, although St. Paul reminds us "no one can say, 'Jesus is Lord,' except by the holy Spirit" (I Cor. 12:3). In Paul's letters, the title "Christ" remains infused with divinity. For Paul, to live was Christ: "I have been crucified with Christ; yet I live, no longer I, but Christ lives in me" (Gal. 2:20).

One commentator points out the interpenetation of person and office in the conjunction of Jesus Christ as the equivalent of one proper name.[4] Christ stands for office, messiahship, mission, faith, and love; Jesus stands for the person who holds office, the messiah, the missionary, the faithful servant, the loving friend. It is the compenetration of God who is love and the man who has love that adumbrates the mystery of Christ Jesus. In him the medium really is the message; the Jesus is the Christ. In Jesus the Christ, self-identity and public role are made as one. Person and word are convertible. The American Indians had the custom of naming their children only after observing some characteristic or gift that made them special. Jesus is saving. Even in the hidden life of Nazareth, Jesus is the anointed one of God, the Christ, who is nonetheless saving the world.

Filium Ejus Unicum

The Latin "filium ejus unicum" means "his only son," or more exactly, his one and only son, his unique son. Jesus is not an adopted son; he is not one of the many holy men of Israel who were called "sons of God" in the Bible. Jesus is Son from the beginning; Jesus is once only; Jesus is unique Son. He remains the only Son, all other sons being dependent in some way upon the only Son. God the Father did not give to humankind a vague and general stewardship of creation in the form of some incarnate role that God would play. God disclosed himself as the Father of the Son, and he cared enough to give us his only Son, the beloved, who emptied himself to become human. St. John speaks poignantly: "For God so loved the world that he gave his only Son, so that everyone who believes in him might not perish but might have eternal life" (3:16). In the gift of Jesus who is the Son of the Father, God has given us God's self, God's personal and intimate life, God's treasure and God's treasures. Such is the ineffable regard of God for us men and women. God has introduced us into the bosom of God's family. God's care for us has not been only instrumental and functional, but also intimate beyond the possibility of being more intimate with a creature who cannot transcend its condition completely, no matter how elevated by grace. Nonetheless, what was possible in love and full disclosure was given without reserve, openly and tenderly, sparing no cost and shrinking from no form of rejection. What is only God's becomes somehow ours in Jesus who is one of us and uniquely one with the Father. Jesus is Immanuel, God-with-us, his only Son. Luke's parable of the Prodigal Son reveals to us that the Father of Jesus remains quintessentially the Father whose love is prodigal.

Let us now consider the five explanatory additions of the Nicene Creed that are not contained in the Apostles' Creed. (1) "The only-begotten Son of God / Born from the Father before all ages" (Filium Dei unigenitum, / qui ex Patre natum ante omnia saecula). (2) "light from light, true God from true God" (lumen de lumine, Deum verum de Deo vero). "God from God" (Deum de Deo), although recited in the Latin liturgy, is a phrase not found in the Niceno-Constantinopolitan Creed, though it is found in local creeds of the same time and place; it is implied in "true God from true God." (3) "Begotten, not made" (genitum, non factum). (4) "Consubstantial with the Father" (consubstantialem Patri); various translations render the Latin "one in substance," "one in essence," or "one in being."[5] (5) "Through whom everything is made" (per quem omnia facta sunt); the reference is to Christ through whom . . . and not to the Father in this context. The biblical source is John's Prologue: "all things came to be through him, and without him nothing came to be" (John 1:3).

The Nicene Creed begins with a small clarification of the wording, "his only son," found in the Apostles' Creed. Properly understood, those three words suffice. What seemed so difficult to comprehend remained how Jesus could be Lord, and the Father could be God, without there being two gods. If Jesus was a super demi-god, the logical contradiction was resolved. No other son was such a son as Jesus, but Jesus was finally a creature of the Father. "His only son" could not specifically address that kind of aberrant theology. The Nicene Creed begins by changing the word "only" (unicum) for the word "only-begotten" (unigenitum). The root of "genitum" is the same as genesis or generation; it implies the opposite of fabricated or made. The first Nicene addition also adds "born of the father," with the same intent to separate itself from "made by the father." "Before all ages" claims that the Son did not have a beginning, as all creation did "in the beginning." The third Nicene addition uses these words quite specifically: "begotten and not made" (genitum non factum). In the Greek the same word *gennethenta* is used to render *natum* in Latin and *genitum*. We would be justified in concluding that *natum* (born) was to be read with the same meaning as *genitum* (begotten or generated). The two Latin words which render the one Greek word are designed to suggest that "generation" proper to the Father and the Son, in direct contrast to the "making" proper to the creation of sons and daughters of the Father Almighty, creator of heaven and earth. Distinctive of the Council of Nicaea, the third addition made the crucial matter clear, and the fourth addition, "consubstantial" (homoousion in Greek) cuts off any possible straddle between divine "generation" and "creation." It was this one word, *homoousion*, that caused so much controversy. Many of the Council Fathers did not wish to put into the creed any words or phrases not already found in the scriptures. To do so seemed to be stepping outside of revelation from God and entering into the philosophies of humanity.

Greek was the language of the church in the East, and the site of this first ecumenical council was located in Asia Minor, somewhat southeast of present-day Istanbul in Turkey. The creed was written in Greek, and the dominant theology and philosophy remained Greek in the East where the church was first and most extensively established. Because the position of Arius held that Jesus Christ was a creation of the Father, exalted far above the human, but short of the divine, the pursuit of *homoousion* as a necessary precision pleased the majority of the Council Fathers.[6] Arian proponents were fond of quoting St. John in such texts as these: "If God were your Father, you would love me, for I came from God" (John 8:42); "Now this is eternal life, that they know you, the only true God, and the one whom you sent, Jesus Christ" (John 17:3); and "Stop holding on to me, for I have not yet ascended to the Father. But go to my brothers and tell them, 'I am going to my Father and your Father, to my God and your God'" (John 20:17). In opposition to the Arian position, the Nicene Creed's additions insist that the Son was eternally begotten (not made), and was *homoousion* (one in being) with the Father. We speak of homogenized milk; *homoousion* means literally the "same (homo) stuff (ousion)." The prologue to John's Gospel gives the scriptural quarry from which many of these creedal rocks were hewn.

Although *homoousion* was subscribed to by the majority of the several hundred signers of the Nicene Creed from East and West in 325 A.D., the controversy did not cease. The Roman Emperor, Constantine, who had convened the Council, hoped they had hammered out a document of irrefragable unity. Actually the term did not become immediately popular or widely quoted. Any term, of course, can be interpreted to mean what the interpreter has already decided to believe. That was the problem with people quoting the same scriptures and meaning contrary things. Nonetheless, *homoousion* became a rallying point for orthodoxy, and it was used more and more in the years between Nicaea (325) and the Council of Constantinople (381), when Athanasius stood against the world.[7]

The Dedication Creed of a provincial council gathered in Constantinople in 341 reflects the general unsureness with *homoousion* in those interconciliar years. For some it was too much, because not in scripture, and for others it was too little because it did not elaborate. Thus this creedal text:

> And in one Lord Jesus Christ, his son, God only-begotten, through whom are all things, who was begotten from the Father before all the ages, God from God, whole from whole, sole from sole, complete from complete, king from king, lord from lord, living Word, living wisdom, true light, way, truth, resurrection, shepherd, door, unchangeable and immutable; invariable image of the deity, essence, purpose, power and glory of the Father, first-born before every creature [*or* of all creation], who was in the beginning with God, God the Word, according to the statement of the Gospel, "And the Word was God"; through whom all things were made and in whom all things consist; who in the last days came down from above. . . .[8]

To construct a foolproof conciliar statement remains difficult. Documents and creeds have to be read in living communities, where group dialogue eliminates deviant meanings. Nonetheless, a series of short yes-or-no questions might facilitate an understanding of the orthodox theology, however proposed. Thus:

> Is there one God? Yes.
> Is the Father God? Yes.
> Is the Son God? Yes.
> Is the Father the Son? No.
> Is the Son the Father? No.
> Did the Father become man? No.
> Did the Son become man? Yes.

The Niceno-Constantinopolitan Creed takes these bald, paradoxical statements of faith and gives some descriptive and systematic explanation of them. Thus one can see how *homoousion* became the magna carta of systematic theology, which introducd the necessary and further elaboration of biblical theology.[9]

Let us summarize what has been said about this second article of the creed. To believe in God the Father, and in Jesus who is Lord already comprises the essence of Christianity. The creed has more to say, of course, and Christianity is very rich in further content. But "Jesus is Lord" would function as a three-word creed if we needed such economy of phrase. The Apostles' Creed had said of Jesus Christ that he was the "only Son." That word *only* (unicum) was elaborated and clarified by four Latin words in the Nicene Creed: *only-begotten* (unigenitum), *born* (natum), *begotten* (genitum), and *consubstantial* (consubstantialem). The Greek used three different words: *monogene* (unigenitum), *gennethenta* (natum and genitum), and *homoousion* (consubstantialem). The implications of the incarnation should come to the reader as a shock, similar to the one perceived in the discussion of the mystery of the One and Many. How can the Nicene Creed add to the Apostles' Creed: "We believe in *one* God and in *one* Lord Jesus Christ"? That sounds like two "one's." And yet there is only one God. And furthermore, how shall we read "True God from true God" without having two Gods? Yet there is only one God, and the Father is God and Jesus is Lord (God). The second article of the creed insists that we believe that Jesus is God, that Jesus is Son, that only the Son became man, and that God is only one. Many compromise positions were advanced that tried to save the logic of the situation. None of them were perduring. The mystery of the incarnation, properly understood, mirrors the immensity and ineffable quality of the mystery of creation. Both mysteries, no doubt, present the infinite and sovereign God, whose Son made human we now shall follow in his story on earth.

Dominum Nostrum

The Latin "Dominum nostrum" means "our Lord." The Hebrews wrote the mysterious and ineffable word for God, which was the sacred tetragrammaton YHWH, but they did not presume to pronounce it. What the vowels might have been, if ever known, were lost to us. When the Hebrew scriptures were read aloud, the Scribes pronounced for YHWH the Hebrew word *adonai* which was a more generic word for God. The Greek translators of the *Septuagint* chose the Greek word *kyrios* to render *adonai*. Where the Hebrew wrote YHWH, they transcribed *kyrios*. The Latin for *kyrios* is *dominus*; the English is

"Lord." The word "Jehovah," came about mistakenly by taking the vowels from the word *adonai* and inserting them in YHWH.[10]

"Jesus is Lord" represents an early Christian confession of faith, well attested to in the scriptures. Yet Jesus himself could quote the *Shema*:

> Jesus answered, "The first is this: 'Hear, O Israel! The Lord our God is Lord alone! You shall love the Lord your God with all your heart, with all your soul, with all your mind, and with all your strength.'" (Mark 12:29–30)

The Christian faith concluded that this same Jesus nevertheless is Lord, not the Father but equal to the Father, as much YHWH as YHWH itself. This man is God; this Jesus is YHWH; this Jesus is creator and pantocrator of the whole universe. For the Jewish Christians it would have bestowed the consummate title to call Jesus the Lord; they heard echoes of the entire Old Testament behind the sacred name. For the Gentile Christians it would have been more adulatory to call Jesus only Son of God; they heard promise of a high Christology that held Jesus to be co-eternal with the Father. In the creed itself there seems to be progression of titles. Because Jesus is the Christ, he is the only Son; because he is the only Son, Jesus is Lord.

Words embody human thoughts, and the inner "word" or concept that embodies our particular insight manifests to us what we have understood in our intellect. From this common human experience we approach the mystery of God, whose Word, the distilled and perfect Word of God, gives full expression to the Father. The Word of God is so full that it constitutes the substance of the Father. The Word is the Father's total self-expression, the perfect reflection of his being, the mirror image that captures not just a surface likeness but the entire essence of the Father, whose essence is to be (esse). This perfect self-expression that is the Father's Word, the Son only-begotten of the Father, became human. In short, when the Father wished to express himself in a created manner, to speak God to an outside as it were, to jump out of God's divine being if it were possible, to be uttered into a void that was nothing without God, to let there be light, the vocabulary thought adequate to express the infinite God in space and time was human nature. Our flesh and bones, the unique amalgam of matter and spirit that is human nature, *we* were God's tongue. Human beings are God's creative vocabulary; we are God's self-expression in creation itself. I try to capture this mystery of God in the following poem:

As it were,
We are God mystery
Turned inside out:
God's self-expression.
Our flesh his words,
Our bones a grammar,
Providence his sentences,
Faith the translation,
Jesus the interpreter.
Our story, God's story,
Jesus says, this day.

From the beginning, from all eternity, the central event of creation from whose still point the universe expands was Jesus Christ our Lord, the infinite Word of God made flesh. From a theological viewpoint, he is the primal and essential "big bang" that sets the universe into being. The perfect expression of the mystery of the One and the Many, that is, the creator who is everything and the creature who is yet something, culminates succinctly and eminently in Jesus of Nazareth born just two thousand years ago. From all eternity the Son was the Father's perfect self-expression; Jesus Christ continues that mystery now expressed in the world. Adam and Eve are but antecedent whispers and Jewish salvation history but prologue. Church history remains but epilogue to this Christ event, and the Kingdom to come is but the sequel to the hub event of all time. God was in Jesus. The fullness of revelation is Jesus. God can reveal no more; God gave us all in Jesus; God said it all in speaking this infinite Word made flesh. There can be no more to say.

Revelation can develop, nonetheless, in this sense. We can come to understand ever more and to apply the mystery of the incarnation more widely to new circumstances. One Christology would have humankind at the center of the universe, and Jesus Christ become human as the remedy to an initial divine plan fallen hostage to perverse human freedom. Such a theology represents a geocentric point of view, wherein the earth is the center and the sun rises and falls on it. A more heliocentric Christology places the Son made human at the center of creation, intended from the beginning, and human beings past and future revolve around the infinite light of that mystery of God's Word made flesh.

Face to face with God in that life to come in eternity, we shall share in an analogous way the union of the Son of God and Jesus.

Hiding our faces from the face of God in the Garden of Eden, we shared in only a diminished way the union of the Many and the One which is celebrated so intensely in this man Jesus who is Lord. Human nature in Adam and Eve was made in the image of God; they were imperfectly but genuinely God's self-expression. Human nature remains god-talk; our meaning constitutes God's vocabulary, prepared for the perfect and loving utterance that is Jesus, who overcomes the limitation of human nature. The blessed in heaven will enjoy this human nature, exalted to the right hand of the Father where sits the flesh of Jesus. And the blessed will share fully in his love and be graced to approach more closely to God than the original happy pair in Eden. Backward and forward in time, Christ constitutes the still center of all creation, conceived from all eternity, born of a woman in a certain moment of our time.

God made many covenants with humankind in the history of leading men and women to be brothers and sisters of Christ. From the promise of a savior given in the Garden, to the Covenant with Abraham, Moses, David, we witness the ever-closing approach of the Word of God among us. God's "I love you" reaches a critical mass, and God's embrace becomes so tight that the Son of God becomes human. In the Son made human the world is given the new and everlasting covenant. In this bond God grasps all of human nature and history. Jesus is the perfect creation, that is not the infinite God and yet in no way is opposed or distant to God. Here is the definitive covenant, of its nature eternal, needing no renewal, subject to no diminution, not even in the death of Jesus. That death was swallowed up in the glorious affirmation of eternal life in the resurrection of Jesus. Now enthroned, the flesh of Jesus is God's irreversible self-bestowal and self-gift. Not subject in glory to change or overthrow, not subject to betrayal from without or change of mind from within, the risen Jesus is the definitive and unsurpassable covenant and bond with God.

Let us call Jesus "irrevocable" and once and for all. So often in an event like a football game, we see with heart sinking, the beautifully executed winning play called back and revoked because of a foul, the athletic equivalent of sin that undoes covenants of old. But praise be to God, the flesh of Jesus cannot be taken back. It is *irrevocable*. The Father has tied his hands, burnt his bridges, married off without possibility of divorce his only Son. We receive the Father's self-expression as a self-gift who is Jesus. God can do no more, and what God has done here cannot be undone. There is no undoing the flesh of Jesus, annihilating or negating his body. For all eternity Jesus sits at the right hand of the Father. Jesus is *irrevocable*. For better or for worse, in sickness or in health, the human race is wed to God. Jesus creates solidarity with all human beings past and future. Jesus is the way to God, the mediator and bridge, the man for all, God-with-us and God-for-us.[11] St. John gives these words of Jesus:

> Now this is eternal life, that they should know you, the only true God, and the one whom you sent, Jesus Christ. I glorified you on earth by accomplishing the work that you gave me to do. Now glorify me, Father, with you, with the glory that I had with you before the world began. (John 17:3–5)

EPILOGUE

Lord of Lords

In the second article, the Son of God made human is declared Lord of lords, and thus our Lord. "His only Son" signifies that Jesus is one being with the Father, of one being with the One. He is God of God, Lord of Lord, light from light, true God from true God.

What is said about us follows. We are his people, in the Lord's Kingdom, under his protection and benevolence. In the humanity of Jesus, our Lord visits us, not as plenipotentiary but as vulnerable infant child of humble stable origin. We receive not strength, but the infinite weakness of God, which turns out to be more than strength. We receive not supervision, but participation. We receive not hierarchy of God and human beings, but intimacy and solidarity with the human predicament. *Jesus is Lord* says to us that God wishes to give God's self and not just the gifts of God. Jesus is the self-gift of God, the *ne plus ultra* revelation of God, the unsurpassable gift of God in God's own godness. Here is the One become the Many, the two in one flesh, the irrefragable marriage of the divine and the human, of the One and the Many, the infinite and the finite.

ARTICLE III

To TURN TO THE third article: "He was conceived by the power of the Holy Spirit, and born of the Virgin Mary." The immediate insight sees Jesus Christ as a miracle of God's power. He was conceived without a human father and born to a virgin mother.

The further insight sees Jesus Christ as more than a miraculous child whose birth exceeds the powers of nature. No miracle birth can be adequate cause for God becoming human. Jesus is indeed beyond the powers of Joseph, but he remains equally beyond all power. No antecedents of history can account for this birth. Here we have more than a miracle. Here we have infinity made vulnerable. The descent of God into mortality beggars all description of power. Here is not only the result of God's power, but precisely the laying of power aside to be born of woman as a helpless infant. Here is only weakness and the evacuation of infinite being and doing. Nursing at the breast of his own creature, Jesus plays before the Father "lovely in the limbs of the children of men." The madonna and child present an icon of the vulnerability that the infinite God is capable of. Who would have dreamed that the enormous God could become so tiny, that the omnipotent ruler of the universe could lie so frail in his mother's arms, looking upon her with the same smile she teaches him, and the same eyes she gave to him.

Qui Conceptus Est de Spiritu Sancto

The Latin "qui conceptus est de Spiritu Sancto" means "who is conceived by the Holy Spirit." The creed affirms that Jesus Christ our Lord stems from the holy spirit of God, which hovered over the waters in the aboriginal creation of the earth made lovely for humankind. This same "spirit" now overshadows Mary, who will then bear a son. Jesus who is Lord, "through whom all things were made," is himself made flesh. But, if Jesus, who is Lord, is Lord of the universe and maker of heaven and earth, his enfleshment cannot be explained as something from below. This Jesus who is sovereign source of all being cannot be derived from Mary and Joseph, who bring a child into the world as all parents do without consulting the child, who remains beholden to them for the wherewithal to strike any attitude at all toward existence. Only the uncreated initiative of God could account for Jesus who is Lord, the Word made flesh.

Although a later theology would see in the words of the creed the Trinitarian Holy Spirit of the Father and Son, originally the third article intended to proclaim only that the holy power of God gives the ultimate explanation of Jesus, whatever his more proximate causes. In a diminished way the conception of Jesus of Nazareth presents a comparison with a popular theology of parenting. Accordingly, the father and mother create the body of the baby into which God infuses an immortal soul. The anthropology underlying this theology may be debatable, but the intent is clear. The eternal person destined to see the face of God cannot be adequately accounted for by the power of physical parents. In a parallel but eminent way, the Holy Spirit overshadows Mary and the child in her womb. She is so graced by God with such sovereign power and infinite love that the child is drawn into God from the moment of conception. Her child is Son of God; the Son of God is her child. No causality in this world can adequately account for the existence of Jesus. No antecedents can explain who he is.

As Adam was made from nothing in the Garden in the beginning, so Jesus is made from Mary, sinless, the being compliant-to-God, the holy and virgin mother. Mary is the new creation and the New Israel; she is the new Eve and the new virgin rib. Her story in the Gospels of Matthew and Luke is told in terms of the Bible and its promises. "Conceived of the Holy Spirit" suggests a new beginning,

50

a new day, a new heaven and earth, and a new Adam. Now is the beginning of the end time; the reign of God on earth approaches. "The kingdom of God is at hand" (Mark 1:15).

The word "conceived" found in the Apostles' Creed is a later addition to the older Roman Creed, which reads "born of the Holy Spirit and the Virgin Mary." That formula suggests co-causality rather than divided causality. The belief, of course, was not and is not that Jesus is half-God and half-man. It is the annunciation in Luke that accounts for the present choice of words in the creed: "Behold, you will conceive in your womb and bear a son" (Luke 1:31). The Nicene Creed does not employ the word "conceived." It speaks not of the first moment of Jesus' existence, but of his enfleshment as the wider mystery: "by the Holy Spirit he was enfleshed from the Virgin Mary and made man" (et incarnatus est de Spiritu Sancto ex Maria Virgine, et homo factus est). The Greek word in the Nicene Creed which corresponds to "enfleshed" is *sarkothenta*, which the Latin translates as *incarnatus*. "Enflesh" is a rather literal anglicization of "incarnate." In contemporary Sunday liturgical usage, "enfleshed" is rendered as "born" of the Virgin Mary. It is probable that the word, "conceived," which carries overtones of the infancy narratives in Matthew and Luke, excludes Joseph more directly than does the phrasing of the Nicene Creed.

How then should "conceived" be read in the creed? In a "new creation" perspective, the word suggests created afresh as in the beginning of time by the sovereign freedom of God. In the "infancy narratives" perspective, the word suggests a miraculous asexual conception. The virgin womb of Mary is made fertile by the sovereign power of God where the power of man to produce life is impotent. Similarly, the women of the Bible too old or infertile to bear children, such as Sarah, Hannah, and Elizabeth, become quickened with child by the word of God, whose promise is always a creative word: "let there be light." Jesus is a miraculous baby, therefore, not unlike the other wonder-children of the biblical stories. God uses the woman as the genuine mothering womb for the God-produced child, and the obstacles of old age or infertility are overcome by the Almighty. None of these biblical births, however, prescinds from the father's role in procreation. In the birth of Jesus, contrarily, the father is not included and explicitly so. A virgin birth is one of a kind in the Bible.

The biology of ancient times would have given the male the seeding role, understood as the life-force, and would have given the woman the receptive and nurturing mother-earth role. A woman was compared to a fertile field; the seed planted in the soil comprised the business of generation. In some sense all mothers were surrogate mothers, the male seed being already a tiny human being seeking a place to implant and grow. Hence God would have created Jesus as an embryo in the womb of Mary. With a more informed biology we would be inclined to say that God took an egg of Mary.[1] We do not know how the chromosomes of the father are to be provided, unless we make that a part of the miracle of Jesus' conception itself. Questions like "Who did Jesus look like?" rise out of such a context. Did he have his mother's features? The doctrine "conceived of the Holy Spirit," however, never gives to God the role of sexual partner in the conception of Jesus. This is no sacred version of Zeus and Leda.[2] Nor has the doctrine given a role to Joseph as the sexual partner of Mary bringing her to conception. And yet there can be no doubt that Jesus is conceived in love. It should be clear that the doctrine is not a sexual account at all. It is a metaphysical account of an event bigger than the primordial creation of the universe. The birth of Jesus creates the focal point in comparison with which all previous creation is prologue and all subsequent history but epilogue. Whether or not a man and woman had sexual intercourse will not finally explain the particular phrase "conceived of the Holy Spirit." That question, however, does arise more appropriately in the second part of the third article, when we discuss the *Virgin* Mary.

Natus Est Ex Maria Virgine

The Latin "natus est ex Maria virgine" means "born from the Virgin Mary." These words sound echoes of Matthew and Luke in the infancy narratives. At stake is that Jesus had a genuine mother and he was a genuine man, body and soul, as human beings who are born of a mother must be. If Jesus is truly born, he is not a phantom or an illusory body. This creedal text wishes to say something about Jesus' condition first of all, and only consequently about Mary's. If Jesus is authentically human, and Jesus is Lord, then Mary as the mother of Jesus is the mother of God (Theotokos). More precisely, she is the mother of the Son of God, Jesus Christ our Lord. If Jesus is not born of Mary, if Jesus is not truly God-become-human, then our union with him is not truly union with God. The Son of God truly become human restates the creedal doctrine of "conceived of the Holy Spirit and born from the Virgin Mary." The correlative of Jesus is Son of God made human remains that Mary be mother of God; they rise and fall together.

The virginity of Mary remains a sacred and cherished part of an ancient tradition in Christendom. It has been almost everywhere and always understood as biological virginity, at least in this restrictive sense that Jesus was not conceived by sexual intercourse with anyone. Yet, virginity has never been prized as solely a biological condition, as if mere intactness was more virtuous than integrity of soul. Rather virginity is prized by Christians because the condition of the body points to the condition of the soul. Accordingly, theological virginity remains more important and more profound, just as the spiritual overshadows the physical. Since the spiritual and the physical combine in human nature, soul virginity and body virginity remain interrelated. Just as an evangelical poverty that expresses trust in God is more valued than a material poverty itself, so an evangelical virginity that takes God alone as the love of one's life is valued more than physical virginity alone.

Faith in God, readiness to do his will, devotion to love and goodness, suggest the heart of virginity in the Bible. Virgin Israel, beloved and covenanted to the One God, must not run after pagan gods, who are adulterous lovers. The Old Testament Israel was elect and chosen; she belonged to a jealous God. Thus the Fathers of the church could talk of Mary conceiving the Lord first in her heart, then in her womb. The Spirit speaks in the ear of Mary attentive to the word of God above all else, and she conceives of the Holy Spirit. "Behold, I am the handmaid of the Lord. May it be done to me according to your word" (Luke 1:38).[3] Jesus himself showed more interest in the disciple than the kinsman: "As he said this, a woman in the crowd raised her voice and said to him, 'Blessed is the womb that bore you, and the breasts that you sucked!' But he said, 'Rather, blessed are those who hear the word of God and observe it'" (Luke 11:27–28).

The phrase, "a young woman ["virgin" in most English translations] shall conceive and bear a son" of Isaiah's oft quoted prophecy (7:14), speaks of a young unmarried woman, presumably a virgin. The *Septuagint* translated the Hebrew word for such a young girl *almah* into a more restrictive term referring to biological virginity *parthenou*. *Virgo* in Latin, and "virgin" in English follow the Greek. Interestingly, the early versions of the creed in English speak of the "maiden Mary," the presumption being again that a maiden is a virgin. What remains perhaps noteworthy is that the infancy narratives of Matthew and Luke mount a collage of Old Testament themes and allusions, including a direct reference to this text of Isaiah. Accordingly, Mary becomes the figure of the New Israel, the mother of the Messiah, the dawn of a new age. The title "Virgin Mary" functions almost as a proper name, just as Christ Jesus combines title and name into a quasi-proper name. Jesus is the new humanity, created from nothingness, that is, from the virginity of Mary, a pure and unadulterated new beginning of the new world. He is pure and she is pure; both are born of God who is pure and simple. Words from Gerard Manley Hopkins' poem, "The Blessed Virgin Compared to the Air we Breathe" come to mind:

> I say that we are wound
> With mercy round and round
> As if with air: the same
> Is Mary, more by name.
> She, wild web, wondrous robe,
> Mantles the guilty globe,
> Since God has let dispense
> Her prayers his providence:
> nay, more than almoner,
> The sweet alms' self is her
> The men are meant to share
> Her life as life does air.[4]

Biblical scholarship has pointed out the inconclusiveness of the Gospel evidence about the Virgin Mary, although Matthew and Luke have not been undermined.[5] The biblical texts alone will not prove the virginity of Mary, largely because the text remains a special and limited kind of history of the events. Some details of the early accounts of Jesus' childhood show theological reconstruction beyond what could be reasonably expected in the redaction of the public life and death of Jesus. Not to prove, however, is not to disprove either. Powerful are the claims of the tradition and the teaching of the church that extol the Virgin Mary in creed and prayer, in song and in cathedral.

Objections have been made that a theology of sexuality that demeans human reproduction as somehow connected with Original Sin, or just the vague shame and guilt that surround sexuality in almost all cultures, has been reinforced by the asexual purity of Mary and the virginal conception of Jesus. At the risk of seeming old-fashioned, I would answer that religion and sexuality do experience an inevitable tension. How can one avoid the universal belief that human nature as we know it lacks integrity? Human actions are flawed by the division suffered between body and soul. Concupiscence or disequilibrium is universally recognized in human sexual behavior. To accept this argument, one need not single out sexuality as the only locus of our sinfulness; it remains simply a battlefield where everyone has lost at some time in their life. "Let the one among you who is without sin be the first to throw a stone at her" (John 8:7) could be said by Jesus because he knew no one would be pitching. The division between heart and head, between body and soul, manifests itself painfully to all men and women sooner or later. Such is the testimony of human experience. When Jesus, who is Lord, dwells so intimately with Mary, should we not understand that she would be at one with God, healed of the divisions of sin, given integrity of body and soul, established in the primordial virgin condition that human nature hopes to achieve before the face of God in heaven, where there will be no birthing because no longer any dying. In short, the virginity of Mary proclaims the fullness of grace and the fulfillment of salvation. This virginity follows upon the pure and consummate wedding of God and humanity, to whom is given the grace of integrity. Mary anticipates our redemption. Her virginity and her integrity remain two sides of the same coin.

The reader might be inclined to agree with the treatment above of the fittingness of a virgin or integral sexuality, if Mary is to lay claim to the fullness of grace. The reader might still ask just what was the actual sexual experience of Mary. I am often tempted to answer this question by asking why it is any of our business to know the private life of any person? Yet, a child is a public matter, and society has the right to know the father. When the child has been compared to God, that interest becomes compelling. What Mary's sexual life might have been before the conception of Jesus, or what it was like after the birth of Jesus is much less our business. Nor do we need to resolve a collateral proposition that Mary gave birth to Jesus in some virginal manner without labor. In giving birth in the stable where the animals were housed, she knew something of the poverty of the flesh. In giving birth to a healthy child, she knew something of the miracle that is birth, unrecognized as such only because it is common. The creed, however, raises none of these peripheral matters. The virginal conception in the creed does exclude Joseph and calls for the intervention of God. It does include Joseph as the adopting father in whose descent from David the child Jesus will be included.

The physical virginity doctrine in the creed depends largely upon the Gospel infancy narratives, and is further supported by centuries of Christian tradition and church teaching. Arguments have been made, even by Christians, that the virginity of Mary is more theological than biological, and that the Gospel stories are far from being without liberal use of metaphor and imagination. Accordingly, the virginal conception is a shorthand for a human conception that later was recognized to be so remarkably graced by God. What is at stake, it is argued, is the ontology of Jesus and not the biology of Mary. Sceptics advance the circumstances of a premature birth, or even conception from rape, incest, or some form of promiscuity. Partheno-genesis in human beings has never been documented, but should it very rarely occur, it would never be given credence. The faith of the Christian community, however, does not favor any of these ingeni-ous explanations.

The Nicene Creed adds a line that gives an account of the rea-son for the incarnation: "Who on account of us human beings and our salvation descended from heaven" (Qui propter nos homines[6] and propter nostram salutem descendit de coelis). Jesus is the Word of God through whom the Father made all that is made. To restore and recre-ate that original creation which had fallen into evil, from which it needed to be rescued by an intervention beyond its own power, Jesus comes to save. St. John writes: "For God so loved the world that he gave his only Son, so that everyone who believes in him might not perish but might have eternal life" (3:16). At the time the Nicene Creed was being formulated, Athanasius wrote a small but beautiful trea-tise, *On the Incarnation,* to explain such a theology of salvation.[7] The descent from heaven also picks up the whole kenosis theology of some-one like St. Paul, who saw the Christ-event as the marvel of the macro-infinite God become a babe at his mother's breast in the micro-world of where the animals lodged.

What can we conclude about the third article of the creed in its entirety? We might say at first that the creed tells us primarily about Jesus Christ, that he is from God, and in the context of the second article that he is divine. It tells us also that Jesus is from Mary, and he should be judged to be fully human. True God and true man is shorthand for "conceived by the Holy Spirit and born from the Virgin Mary." So runs the third article that heads the list of the *gesta Christi* (the deeds of Christ) that follow. According to the Apostolic witness, these are the historical Gospel deeds of Christ that reveal Jesus is Lord.

Doctrine about Mary's condition remains a secondary consid-eration, although intertwined. Tradition and church teaching have affirmed the "virgin birth," more properly called the virgin concep-tion. That doctrine, however, has not been proposed as central to Chris-tianity and crucial for salvation, even though it has been celebrated in season and out. The historical record is not unanimous, yet the trend toward affirmation is clear. Not all the early creeds make men-tion of Mary at all. The Nicene Creed as issued by the Council of Nicaea, the first ecumenical council, does not mention the Virgin Mary. Faith was lodged in the confession of the Father, the Son, and the Holy Spirit. Through the recent centuries Protestant theologians have been more liberal in their interpretation of the "virgin birth," and Catholics more conservative.

Granted that Jesus is the subject of the creedal affirmations, what can secondarily be said about Mary? Given Mary is a virgin mother, that does not prove Jesus is God. Given Mary is not a virgin mother, that does not prove Jesus is not God. Mary's virginity proves nothing except that a miracle has happened. A miraculous conception cannot prove Jesus is Son of God, but only that he is wonderful. Nor can we prove Jesus is not the Son of God even if he were conceived as other children. Our belief in the divinity of Jesus rests on the testimony of the resurrection. Nor could we prove to a skeptic that being born of a virgin woman comprises adequate proof of one's full humanity. Jesus should not be presented as demi-God, half-God and half-man because of mixed parentage; we are not talking about the miraculous seed of any God.

Too much can be claimed for the virginity of Mary. She is not holy merely because she is virgin; she is not virgin because she is holy. Mary's holiness stems from her complete faith in God. Her bodily condition remains remarkably unknowable to us. Only weak argument can be made that Mary actually told the disciples the circumstances of the birth of Jesus. The Gospel accounts of the later years of Jesus and Mary seem to belie such knowledge or communication on her part. Moreover, her bodily condition in any precise terms, that are no invasion of her privacy, remains not crucial to Jesus being Lord nor to Mary being sinless.

Nevertheless, why would anyone want to deny the virginity of Mary? The historical record can hardly prove nor disprove the matter. The Christian tradition and the church teaching remain overwhelmingly in its favor. The beauty of the familiar story of Jesus and Mary has struck poet and artist throughout the centuries.

Feminist objections to the virginity of Mary center on the dysfunction that Mary presents as a role model for women who are mothers and not virgins, and virgins who are not mothers. The feminist objection points out that motherhood is not for all women, and neither is a virginal sexuality. Mary as ideal seems to put women on a pedestal, and the outcome is not so much to honor women as to marginalize them from the business and rough and tumble of the world.

The details of the life of Mary, however, need not be so opposed to the honorable goals of contemporary feminism. Today's objection leans upon the story of Mary as overly meek and unworldly as customarily presented by commentators on the brief scriptural mentions of Mary. Suppose one were to read the scriptures in a way more sympathetic. Thus, Mary first appears as an unwed woman who chooses to keep her child. Her fiancé is informed that she thinks she has a god-given vocation that she must follow regardless of his career plans. Moreover, he must trust her expression of her sexual life as she presents it to him. He must adapt to her vocation as woman and mother in her own way. She gives birth to her firstborn child in a stable without the presence of any midwifery. When the adolescent boy Jesus disobeys his parents, she disciplines him: "Son, why have you done this to us? Your father and I have been looking for you with great anxiety" (Luke 2:48). In Jesus' public life it is Mary who takes leadership and charge of the wedding crisis in Cana: "They have no wine" (John 2:3). At the foot of the cross his mother stands fearless with a few other women, all the men having run away. In the church council of Pentecost Sunday, Mary takes her place with the men in the upper room awaiting the descent of the Holy Spirit and the empowering for mission in the church that it will bring. Here is a picture of no unreal or marginalized woman.

I believe whatever the church teaches about the virginity of Mary, although I also believe that such teaching must be interpreted, as all doctrine must be, in the context in which it was developed. Moreover, I believe a deepening of our understanding of this beautiful doctrine could occur, and that that further appreciation might appear to some as a "change." "Conceived of the Holy Spirit and born from the Virgin Mary" remains a biblical and creedal shorthand for the blessed mystery of God made flesh whose inner dimensions we do not know as scientists who probe an event in and of this world. Jesus originates from God; Jesus is from above. His birth is not a variant on the Tower of Babel story, wherein humankind tries to lift itself by its own bootstraps. Joseph, as a sexed being, was born and will die; he represents the limitations of nature and the helplessness of history. Salvation is not from below but from above. Grace is from God; Jesus is the great sacrament; Jesus is from above. Joseph is impotent to sow life in its profound dimensions; he is an adoring spectator in the story, just as the shepherds who listen to the angels sing: "Glory to God in the highest." Jesus appears resourceless in the crib and on the cross; he tastes what the dependency of the creature to sustain life is like. He knows not the impotency that sin creates, but he knows the poverty of the human condition. Nonetheless, Jesus is from above, "conceived by the power of the Holy Spirit and born of the Virgin Mary," and he will be raised up to the right hand of the Father.

In the first article of the creed, God puts outside of God's infinity the Many that is all of creation. Outside of God meant without God in some way, and without God entailed being without life. In the second and third articles, God puts inside of God's infinity the Many that is all of creation. God draws Mary to within, and the union is so close that the Son of God becomes her child and the whole creation's child. Inside God's embrace now means with God in some way, and with God brings eternal life. "Conceived by the power of the Holy Spirit and born of the Virgin Mary" remains a variant expression of the mystery of the One and the Many. The infinite God is all that exists; the creature yet somehow exists and is drawn back to God. Articles three through seven describe this embrace of Creator and creature, how small and deep it was implanted, and how large and wide the Lord's arms stretched out on the cross until he comes again.

EPILOGUE

Lord of Nature

In the third article, the Son of God is declared Lord of nature. His human nature is conceived of God and born of woman. The lordship of God over the human body is reflected in the virgin conception. No antecedents of nature are necessary to God, and none are adequate to account for the mystery of the Word made flesh. In the cooperation and compliance of Mary, which allows her to be called truly the mother of God, the creed declares that God is both lord of the human body and of the human heart. Lord of nature, Lord of love, Lord of human birth, once again, Lord in the beginning.

What is said about us follows. The origin of humanity remains God's idea and the fruit of God's love for us. We were a gleam in God's eye before we ever came to be. God loved humanity before it existed. God thinks of us always, sustains us by his love, holds us in the palm of her hand. We are never on our own, from our own, never parthenogenetic, never our own source. We are thus God's children, born of God ultimately, belonging to God and but lent to human parents. We are sojourners on this earth, destined for our home with God, where our being originated and to which it tends day and night.

ARTICLE IV

To TURN TO THE fourth article: "He suffered under Pontius Pilate, was crucified, died, and was buried." The immediate insight sees the terrible passion of Jesus Christ as a revelation of the extent of his love for humankind. How wicked must be our sinfulness, and how compelling must be God's love in Jesus to endure so heavy a cross. Suffering must be the price of atonement for sin. By the cross humanity is redeemed or bought back from the powers of evil. Now are the gates of heaven reopened. In the blood of the Lamb we are all washed.

The further insight does not find so much an explanation for suffering in the passion, but rather a demonstration of the Son of God's willingness to join us on the cross of this world's agony. Beyond comprehension, God died. God is not dead, but God truly died. No imagination could have guessed the extent of God's belittlement. God died. The suffering was not make-believe; God suffered. That God suffered and died remains an awful mystery. Moreover, Jesus' death results not from the predicament of an impotent providence; the cross was a God-given vocation. The mystery of suffering may not be so much the price divine justice demands, but rather the cost of a love that would not let go its embrace, even when the beloved was unworthy and hateful. The cross reveals how we are death-dealing and God remains life-giving.

Passus sub Pontio Pilato, Crucifixus, Mortuus, et Sepultus

The Latin "passus sub Pontio Pilato, crucifixus, mortuus, et sepultus" means "suffered under Pontius Pilate, was crucified, died, and was buried." In the earliest account of the passion and resurrection proclamation, Paul writes to the Corinthians a four-part evangel: "Now I am reminding you, brothers, of the gospel I preached to you, which you indeed received and in which you also stand. Through it you are also being saved, if you hold fast to the word I preached to you, unless you believed in vain. For I handed on to you as of first importance what I also received: that Christ *died* for our sins in accordance with the scriptures; that he was *buried*; that he was *raised* on the third day in accordance with the scriptures; that he *appeared* to Kephas, then to the Twelve" (1 Cor. 15:1–5, emphasis added). Nowhere in Paul does he tell of the active ministry of Jesus, or even show knowledge of or interest in the events that preceded the Last Supper. It is the paschal mystery, the Christ-event, that rivets Paul's attention; the incarnation, the passion, the resurrection and glorification of Jesus contain the meaning of the graciousness of God. The creed proceeds in the same direct fashion. From the birth of Jesus from Mary, we jump to the death of Jesus by Pilate. Everything in between is implied. In the creed, Jesus makes a brief entrance and a swift exit. However succinctly, all the mystery of Jesus is given in his beginning and in his ending.

In this fourth article, the creed adds to the Pauline text the words, "suffered" and "crucified." To the Old Roman Creed our present Apostles' Creed adds "suffered" and "died." It would seem these additions act as emphasis, and a guard against possible improper understanding. The crucifixion involved genuine suffering of the genuine body of Jesus who was truly a man. To the Gnostics and Docetists, for example, it was a scandal that God should suffer. They speak of the apparent suffering of Jesus. But, according to the creed, if Jesus was Lord, the Lord God suffered. Furthermore, his burial presupposed genuine death, not just the body's death, not make-believe or apparent death. Jesus who is Lord died and was buried. In short, in suffering he was crucified, and quite dead he was buried. The Niceno-Constantinopolitan Creed omits "dead" from this article.

The Latin *passus* which means to undergo pain (passion), is rendered in English as "suffered." The root of that word is to bear under.

Jesus underwent the full penalty of the law that condemned him to crucifixion; he was not spared any of the physical, mental, or spiritual anguish that was a part of that sentence. He suffered the punishment imposed. Far from being insulated from pain because of his godliness, Jesus may well have been more acutely conscious of the terrible predicament of his tortured mind and body. When Pilate leads Jesus forth to show the crowd the beaten and bloody man—*Ecce homo!*[1]—humanity looks upon itself. This is what we do to one another and ultimately to ourselves. We mangle our bodies and the image of God that we are. The worst imaginable sin for the Judeo-Christian imagination would be to strike God, the infinite source of all that exists. Insofar as that was a possiblity, humanity puts to death the Lord of life, Jesus who is the Christ.

The Greeks could imagine no greater crime than the incest of Oedipus, who kills his father and marries his mother. Sophocles knows no greater horror, and he can find little forgiveness except in the apotheosis of Oedipus at Colonnus, where the suffering and blind man seems to earn some reversal of fortune from the justice of the gods.[2] In contrast, Jesus on the cross says: "Father, forgive them, they know not what they do" (Luke 23:34). Humankind is lifted up into God's place as the beloved son now, and the Son of God is cast down in humanity's place into that death which is the wages of sin against God. The passion of Jesus reveals humanity at its worst and God at God's best.

Jesus in his suffering is abandoned: "He saved others; he cannot save himself" (Mt. 27:42). Deserted by his disciples and friends, who are afraid, Jesus is seemingly even abandoned by God: "My God, my God, why have you forsaken me?" (Mark 15:34). The cross remains a scandal; God in heaven remains silent. The man-for-others, as Jesus has well been described, dies with no one for him and no one with him. Judas is against him; Peter denies even knowing him. All the men run away; the women alone remain to mourn and bury him. In giving the Son, God gave us not one gift among many, God gave us the gift of self. God gave us everything in the Son. In Jesus put to death, God died.

In the passion, God does not give humanity a verbal explanation of the mystery of evil and the intolerable injustice of human history, a world of scandal where soft, vulnerable flesh is tormented by accident, fire, sword, famine, illness, and deliberate torture. Hegel calls human history a "butcher's block."[3] God does not justify these terrible ways with humankind by means of words. Jesus who is Lord hangs on the cross with us. We receive a demonstration of solidarity with human pain. God does not spare the only Son, the beloved, from undergoing the dark night of the human condition, the gruesome record of *homo lupus homini*.[4] Far from second thoughts about the value of this idiotic world, full of "sound and fury," God enters the agony with his own flesh. No artist better captures this drama of a world crucified and Jesus crucified along with us and beside us every day than Georges Rouault in his "Miserere" drawings. To be human for Rouault is to undergo daily suffering in this world; to be man or woman is to be at the mercy or non-mercy of others. It is to know the fragility of a human being and the spectre of death hovering over one's shoulder all the time. To be human is to share the passion of Jesus who shares the passion of humankind. *Ecce homo!* Behold the man.

Jesus died in all likelihood on a cross slightly taller than a man's height, his ankles pierced together by one nail which forced his feet to turn sideways. His arms were either nailed through the wrists to support his weight, or roped to the crossbeam, which he was forced to carry to a location just outside the city walls. Golgotha was possibly an old quarry, where there remained an outcropping of rock that formed a stony hill, perhaps resembling a skull in popular imagination.[5] Luke writes: "When they came to the place called the Skull, they crucified him and the criminals there, one on his right, the other on his left" (23:33). In pictorial renditions of the crucifixion, a skull is sometimes positioned at the foot of the cross. Legend carried the story that the Garden of Eden was once located where Jesus was crucified on Calvary. The skull of Adam, which recapitulates the fate of all humanity, is there bathed in the blood of Jesus and thus baptized into eternal life. On that "Good Friday," however, Jesus died naked and taunted by a callous and hostile crowd without pity. He died a slow and lingering death from bleeding, shock, and asphyxiation that comes from the ever more difficult lifting of one's chest to breathe when the weight of one's body is hung. The Evangelists tell it in some detail; it was an abominable torture for any human being. That God should endure it defies imagination.

As a symbol the cross teases our minds with the vertical and horizontal arms that encompass all directions. The cross suspends Jesus, who is lifted up like humankind that hangs in torment between heaven and earth. His arms outstretched to the horizons of this space-time world create a human solidarity. Beside him "the criminals there, one on his right, the other on his left." We Christians hang the cross around our necks and center it on the walls. Accustomed as we are to its shape, it hardly shocks as it once did. The image of the "electric chair" would make us cringe should we mount a ten-foot model above

our altars. The crucifixion is an obscene abomination. Paul alludes
to Deuteronomy when he repeats, "Cursed be everyone who hangs
on a tree" (Gal. 3:13). To be crucified was not only to be tortured, but
to be shamed and humiliated. Roman citizens were protected by law
from this punishment. Crucifixion was fitting for slaves and conquered
people guilty of crime. And yet, Christians proclaim the cross now
as a following of Christ and a way of life. What could one ever find
to give meaning to such a debacle?

The cross borrows its light from the resurrection sun that
brightens the night into day. Nonetheless, one can ask why the cross?
Why not another death for Jesus? Athanasius comments that a death
from weakness and old age would have detracted from Jesus as Lord.
Since death comes in the end for every man and woman, Jesus must
lay down his life in an unambiguous manner.[6]

Another explanation of the cross would have Jesus fall victim
to the abuse of human freedom. Neither he nor his Father can ma-
nipulate human freedom. Although they deplore this sinful human
condition that leads to the cross, they remain impotent to intervene
in human history. This position, however, does not account for the
sovereign providence of the Lord of history, who created freedom and
moves it from within, yet in no way undoing its integrity. For the sovereign God, history is a tool of God's purposes, and the cross is the
God-given vocation of Jesus, rather than a predicament imposed by
his humanity.

A more classical theology of the cross presents Jesus as the victim. He is the lamb, altar, and priest of God. His sacrifice redeems
the world and expiates our sins. Jesus restores the divine order, redresses the divine justice, and re-creates the earth so that it may follow the will of God in an obedience that leads now to life and not
to death. By his death, death itself is overcome. Because the Lord of
the living was put to death and rose again, the death of all of us, brothers and sisters of Jesus, has been undercut in principle. "Where, O
death, is your sting?" (1 Cor. 15:55). Like the bee's barb, the sting is
left in the flesh of Jesus, and death has been disemboweled in its ultimate strike that it thought would be the death of the Lord of life.
As it turns out, ironically, instead of everyone succumbing to death,
death alone finally dies. The apparent victory of death on the cross
remains the death of death once and for all.

Two things remain attractive about this traditional theology of
the cross. (1) It recognizes sin as sin against God. The "no" to life that
constitutes sin, the self-enclosed refusal to give oneself to the true,
the just, the good, and the beautiful, remains at bottom a refusal of

the personal love of God, for which we are destined and to which the things of this world are encoded invitations. Because we actually live in a world of sin and grace, of a "no" or a "yes" to the offer of God's intimate friendship and self-gift, what a dignity and beauty come over everyday life and all of human history. Our decisions involve God ultimately; choices are about eternity; everything is at stake and life presents high drama from the crib to the grave. (2) How good of Jesus to intervene in our behalf. Jesus redresses the injustice done to God whenever God's love is scorned, for God indeed gives us more than a deistic management contract of a distant creator. If love unrequited is always painful, imagine that an infinite love unrequited requires an appropriate reconciliation, a self-gift in return, an equal love in a reciprocal donation. Only Jesus who is Lord could address God so intensely; he did so for our sake. Thus Jesus redeems us and atones for our sins. He reconciles the estranged love of mankind and God, which had gone astray from the original Adam and is restored by the new Adam, who on the cross offers us the fruit of the true tree of life. Salvation history is thus fulfilled and never to be undone, because of the unsurpassable response of Jesus who is human and divine.

The shortcoming of this theology appears in this. God the Father seems hard to please; God seems inaccessible and even pitiless, requiring the sacrifice of the beloved Son in order to placate the injured divinity. Expiation, redemption, cost, and pain, all this theological metaphor seems not to describe the prodigal father who takes the homecoming younger son to his breast with a sign of relief and a ring for his finger and shoes for his feet. This explanation may talk too much of an angry God and of the price of atonement — a pound of flesh. In the Gospels, the Father of Jesus seems to want only to give; the Father has nothing of his own to protect; the Father threatens no punishment that must be undergone to restore God's love.

An alternative theology maintains Jesus as the victim who saves us, but as our victim rather than the Father's victim. It is not the Father who is demanding and who must be reconciled with us. It is we who are angry and alienated; we need to be reconciled with God. Jesus is thus the victim of love's demands. He pays the ransom, but not of God's wrath, but rather of humankind's own pent-up fury. The cost does not entail the restitution of the injured dignity of God who will have only a royal sacrifice, but rather the humble and non–self-serving embrace of a love that does not count the cost. Sebastian Moore's *The Crucified Jesus is No Stranger* seems to me a poetic and insightful explanation of such a theology.[7] Many of my own remarks borrow from his poignant writing.

Accordingly, the human condition is defined as an ego-protective defensive entanglement. Our neuroses as well as our cultural achievements are judged as largely a coping with the fear of death that haunts all conscious flesh. Our ego-projects are the contingent creature's strategy to forestall death, as if that were possible. The vulnerability of the flesh seeks protection from the all-aware eye of the spirit, that grasps in an instant of intuition how intolerable it is to be human and mortal. Thus afraid to be self-giving or trustful in God, because we might not be protected from death and suffering that so threatens us, humanity constructs a pattern of withholding, of ego-defenses, of cultural camouflage that masks the "no" to life and love's demands.[8]

In this theology of the cross, humanity is like a panic-stricken swimmer whom the lifeguard comes to save. In fear the swimmer puts a stranglehold upon its savior. Thus we drag Jesus down to death with us. The lifeguard-savior dies knowingly for love of us. Going down to death embracing us, Jesus unlocks our paralyzed fears and raises us to new life with him. Similarly, the child who is angry and unreconciled with its mother might, in its fear and frustration, flail with its fists the mother who holds it for protection in her arms. Once she absorbs the abuse, however, the anger of the child is spent. When her response to her child's unlovable behavior is an unconditional embrace, the child can break down its ego-defenses in a tearful recognition of the mother's love. Both of them will thus come to recognize that at bottom the child's heart is breaking with pent-up and misdirected love for her. The child is a tangled lover. And so are we all.

The animal that is wounded will bite the hand that comes to save it. Caught in a trap, it assumes that the hand that approaches to release it will only add to its pain. The helping hand may be judged to threaten rather than to protect. Only the rescuer who will take the sting and anger upon his or her own hands will save the animal's life. In the attempt to help, the rescuer may be injured, because of the misdirected fear and panic of the injured creature in a bind of pain that it cannot understand and faced with a savior whose intent it cannot recognize. In our rage and fear over our own dying, we inflict a death blow on Jesus who came to undo our painful trap and heal our mortal wounds. The lance thrust into the side of Jesus on the cross issues in blood and water of the sacraments of reconciliation. The acceptance of that blow is the paradigm of sacrificial love. Jesus accepts to be pierced and he returns good for evil. The cross is the rape of God, who suffers our violence, but also surrenders to us in the knowledge that underneath the hatred lies the frightened and love-deprived human creature faced with its own vulnerability and dread of death. Human beings are indeed tangled lovers, who wound in their own thrashing about those who would save them.

Humanity is loveless and self-serving in the crucifixion of Jesus. The cross represents the infected boil of human sinfulness brought to a head and to a therapeutic condition in the awful killing of Jesus. He is the innocent man, whose good and loving life is so maddeningly out of reach of the sinner. Jesus as victim of love brings sinners the recognition that they are tangled lovers. On the surface they are tied in knots by neurotic and sinful strategies of loveless self-serving that they think will protect their life from death in the absence of God. At bottom they yearn for God with hearts made for loving. In this theology of the cross, God does not just bring good out of evil, but God transforms our self-hatred and brings healing from within our sins. The cross is redemption from below. We think if anyone really knew us, they could not love us. But God comes to embrace us in our helpless and vindicative worst, not despite our sinfulness but because of it. We are the frog the prince must kiss. And in that kiss of death the prince must take to himself the ugliness of death that his embrace takes away. Jesus takes our pain and death into his own body, calming our troubles as he did the storm at sea. Isaiah writes of the "suffering servant": "But he was wounded for our transgressions, he was bruised for our iniquities; upon him was the chastisement that made us whole, and with his stripes we are healed" (53:5).

Not only does the crucified Jesus truly die on the cross, he also was buried. His death was not momentary nor illusory. He truly died, and he was buried as are the dead. His body was given to the earth; he *was buried*. In the creed there is no implicit information about the empty tomb in this phrase. Rather, *was buried* proclaims that Jesus indeed died and his body indeed was entombed. Paul, who proclaims without doubt the resurrection, announces that Jesus *was buried*, but nowhere does Paul narrate the story of the empty tomb.

"Sub Pontio Pilato." Jesus suffered "under Pontius Pilate." The Roman Procurator is the third proper name in the creed. He stands in the place of every sinful human being. Mary, sinless virgin, brings about the birth of Jesus and the victory of the city of God, the kingdom of justice. Pilate, sinful compromiser, brings about the death of Jesus and the seeming triumph of the city of man, the kingdom of injustice. Pilate is not just a one-man villain in the story; he represents humanity. This world abounds with Pilates. There is no justice in this world, where the innocent are punished and the wicked set free. Pilate stands for injustice, for that might that becomes right, in the ways of a sinful world. His decision to condemn is expedient; his judgment is crass and cruel. Jesus falls into the hands of the powers of this world. He is thrown under them, *sub*-jected to Pontius Pilate. Jesus is the all holy and wholly innocent lamb of God, the true son of the Father, in comparison with whom the criminal Bar-abbas (son of the father) represents in an ironic play on words the renegade son for whom Jesus is laying down his life.

At a moment in time that can be dated somewhere between 26–36 A.D. from historical records, Pilate judges guilty the infinite judge of earth and heaven. He knows Jesus innocent and thereby guilty. It is Pilate himself along with all of us who stand trial. Jesus stands mute, Lord of history, but condemned before a petty and insecure Roman official. Two thousand years of Covenant glory—"I will be your God and you will be my people"—culminate in the priests of David's city handing over the Messiah and hope of Israel to the heathen to be tortured to death. To their hated Roman occupation government they accuse Jesus of pretending to be the king of the Jews. It is all so absurd, so tragic, so ironic, so beyond human comprehension.

The Nicene Creed adds to this article a brief phrase by way of giving motivation for the mystery of the cross. The Latin "pro nobis" is rendered in English as "for us" or "for our sake" he suffered. The Latin preposition *pro* and the Greek *huper* make it clear that Jesus was not crucified *because of* us, which would be *propter* in Latin and *dia* in Greek. Rather Jesus dies on our behalf, or "for" us. This short phrase gives a clue which we tried to pursue above, where the cross was seen, not as the imposition of uncontrollable human freedom, but rather as the Father's mysterious will and as a vocation accepted. Paul's early account of the Gospel teaching is quite explicit. "For I handed on to you as of first importance what I also received: that Christ died for our sins in accordance with the scriptures" (1 Cor. 15:3). Probably Paul should be read as claiming that Jesus *died* according to the scriptures, rather than affirming in this earliest proclamation of the resurrection that *for our sins* is according to the scriptures. The creed reflects a later theology of atonement that was indeed found in the scriptures, but was probably not part of the earliest simple account of the resurrection.[9] "No one has greater love than this, to lay down one's life for one's friends" (John 15:13).

EPILOGUE

Lord of Matter

In the fourth article, the creed declares that Jesus suffered, that he fell under the weight of gravity, that he was further burdened with injustice, that he was tortured, and that he died prematurely. Moreover, he was put into the ground, his body was encaved behind an immovable rock. All matter is subject to gravity; all body is subject to going down; all life must be buried in the earth. In suffering, made worse by injustice, Jesus dies as all men and women die. He is big enough to be small, strong enough to be weak, alive enough to die. Nonetheless, Jesus is Lord of matter, and his victory and sovereignty over the grave follows upon his full acceptance of the human condition.

What is said about us follows. What goes down will rise; what dies will live. Matter is not to be loathed; death is not to be feared. Gravity is not sovereign; spirit is all powerful. We do not have any adequate explanation of human suffering, but we do have a demonstration of solidarity. Jesus who is Lord is not reluctant to experience human nature in its material condition. God has no second thoughts, no intent to flood us away again. The Son of God enters matter, takes up flesh, abides in suffering, goes down into the pit. We should not fear our bodies, nor despair our death. We can now be patient in our suffering, for it all belongs to the Lord. Jesus is Lord of matter, for God is Lord of all.

ARTICLE V

To TURN TO THE fifth article: "He descended to the dead." The immediate insight sees the generosity of the Savior who goes even to the depths of the underworld in his dying, and who raises up the just of past ages in his harrowing of hell. In this descent we recognize the communion of Jesus Christ with the dead as well as with the living, with those who have gone before as well as those who will follow.

The further insight sees the descent as the triumph of God over all that is dark and absurd in the world. Jesus is Lord even of the absurd.[1] Jesus knows no dark depth that his life-giving being cannot penetrate. His ingress is everywhere. The infinite resourcefulness of God should outweigh all human fear and all anxiety. Whatever the hellishness we have made or can worry about, Jesus who is Lord, precedes us in victory.

Descendit ad Inferna (Infernos)

The Latin, "descendit ad inferna" means "he descended into the underworld." Jesus descended into hell. Some translations prefer "he descended to the dead." If one follows the Latin "inferna," he literally went down into the inferior or infernal regions. If one follows the Latin "infernos," he descended to the people who have gone down. Jesus went to that universal underworld of the dead. It does not seem the variance in the manuscripts bears much significance; the underworld place and the underworld people would seem to mutually imply one another. Some manuscripts give *infera* instead of *inferna*. The root meaning of both Latin words is "lower." The English word "infernal," however, carries a connotation of punishment, which the word "inferior" does not. Thus, infernal region differs from inferior region in English usage. Regardless of the variant readings, however, there remain several interpretations of what "hell" refers to.

The "descent into hell" concludes the death announcement of Jesus and introduces the resurrection proclamation. The text looks backward to the fourth article on the passion and death, and it looks forward to the Easter affirmation of the sixth article. Jesus' victory over death reaches all the way back in time and down to the bottom of space, in order to recapitulate the history of the world and lift up all things to himself in his resurrection. Therefore he must really go down in death, in order to rise from the bottom of death to the very top of life. In a narrative theology, Jesus died on Friday, and on Saturday he roams the underworld, just as any human being who must undergo what the dead must undergo. But, there in triumph, Jesus liberates the dead of all previous ages. On Sunday morning he rises again (back) from the dead. The space-time dimensions of this narrative reflect an image-laden account. Above and below, before and after, are terms that do not completely explain the eternal-life quality of Jesus' exaltation. Imbedded in that metaphorical narrative, however, there remain a theology and a belief we wish now to explore.

First of all, it should be noted that whereas the Nicene Creed usually amplifies the Apostles' Creed with further explanation, in this instance there is a lacuna. The "descent into hell" is not found in the Eastern Creed, although it was a doctrine neither unheard of nor under attack. Moreover, it is not found clearly in the New Testament, and even less so in the Gospels. The First Letter of Peter speaks of

Jesus after his death: "he also went to preach to the spirits in prison, who had once been disobedient while God patiently waited in the days of Noah" (3:19). Some commentators, however, feel that the reference is directed more to the then popular Book of Enoch, in which the fallen angels were imprisoned in a sub-heavenly hell.[2] Thus, the lordship of Jesus and the redemption of the risen Christ reaches even to the outer limits of the cosmos. Just as Jonah was three days in the belly of the whale in the depths of the sea (Mt. 12:40), the soon-to-rise Jesus was present with power throughout the apocalyptic universe of popular Jewish writings of that time. Other passages are given as possible references to the descent into hell, such as: "Amen, amen, I say to you, the hour is coming and is now here when the dead will hear the voice of the Son of God, and those who hear will live" (John 5:25). Nevertheless, the scriptural basis for the "descent into hell" remains weak. Many, if not all, of such passages show a context that does not clearly and directly confirm the creedal doctrine.[3]

Furthermore, the "descent" is absent from the Old Roman Creed, from which the Apostles' Creed, as we now have it, descended. Its appearance in creeds of importance dates from the fourth century, when it appears in the Fourth Formula of Sirmium (Synod of Sirmium, 359 A.D.) attributed to the Syrian Mark of Arethusa.[4] It is later found in the Creed of Aquileia as quoted by Rufinus.[5] This is the same Rufinus who spread the account of the twelve apostles each adding an article to form the Apostles' Creed. According to Priminius, who wrote some centuries later, it was Philip who contributed "the descent into hell."[6]

Martin Luther thought that the "descent into hell" spoke of the crucified Jesus in death-throes, rather than the resurrected Jesus. For Jesus on the cross, hell thus consisted in being forsaken and abandoned by God. Jesus was forlorn even unto death. That lack of relationship with God is hell. If theologians speak of hell as essentially the loss of God, then Jesus experienced on the cross the seeming abandonment of hell. The dark night of his soul, the all-aloneness of his last hour, this was hell. Our contemporary world that knows the atrocious violence of the twentieth century and the concomitant loss of faith in God might easily identify with this experience of night and being in hell without God. Hell is death, when death is loneliness without God. Hell is death without any loved one who can accompany the dying person and keep the face of love alive. Hell is solitary confinement. Into that hell, Jesus descends.

Two traditional readings have been given to the "descent." The first reads "hell" as a generic term for the underworld. This hell is the Hades of the Greeks and the Sheol of the Hebrews. It is the pit, the grave, the hole in the ground where the body is buried, the bottomless cavity into which the dead are swallowed up. Etymologically the word "hell" is related to the Old German word *holle*, to which the English conceal or hide away is related. The infernal regions are the inferior ones, the lower regions, the underworld down below. Here all human beings are leveled in death, covered over, and sooner or later forgotten. Here all is dark and life as we know it ends. Those who abide in hell cling to a tenuous life, a bodily but bloodless condition that gives them neither joy nor vitality. They are the shadows of their former selves; they comprise the shades of the dead. To them Odysseus in his journey to Hades brings bowls of blood for them to drink, in order to give them strength enough for even brief speech.[7] Abandoned, bereft of life, the dead lie in an underworld dark and dreary. Even worse is the condition of the unburied, who cannot rest in Hades until their body is put under ground. Jesus was indeed not left on the cross to be the prey of wild animals. The creed follows the Gospels which are explicit; he was buried. By a special permission obtained from Pilate, the body of Jesus was quickly laid in a new rock-hewn grave in a garden. Once buried Jesus descended into hell where all the dead must go.

What this reading of a generic hell says is this: Jesus really died. Whatever happens to all human beings in death, wherever they go, whatever they then undergo, it all happened to Jesus. His solidarity remains with all the dead, the past generations and countless multitude of the moribund. Jesus died for everyone and his death is every human being's. In short, God is with those who are in such hell. Whatever the hell it is, God knows all about it.

A second reading, which adds to what has already been said, would interpret the "descent into hell" as the triumphal entry of Jesus into the devil's own kingdom. This is a more specific hell, the Gehenna of the New Testament. This hell is a place of punishment for the wicked, a place of fire and waste like the smoldering garbage-dump landfill outside the city of Jerusalem, which was associated with the pagan abominations in the valley of Gehenna leading to the Kidron valley near Jerusalem. *Gehenna* is derived from the Hebrew *gehinnom*, which means valley of Hinnom. It was located west and south of Jerusalem. The valley of Hinnom was the site of Topheth (Aramaic for place of fire) where human sacrifices were offered by fire to pagan deities (2 Chron. 28:3 and 33:6). Jeremiah condemned Topheth to an eventual destruction (Jer. 7:31–32 and 19:6), and King Josiah destroyed the infamous place (2 Kings 23:10). Hence Gehenna brings associations of a place of sinful abominations, prophetic judgment, and subsequent fiery destruction.[8] This is a place of torment, like the Tartarus of the Greek world, the Inferno of Dante, the Gehenna that is of the damned in the customary heaven and hell contrast of the New Testament. Mark refers to a final punishment of going "into Gehenna, into the unquenchable fire" (9:43). Matthew speaks of a "fiery furnace" (13:42) and "eternal fire prepared for the devil and his angels" (25:41). Revelation describes "the fiery pool burning with sulphur" (19:20), the "pool of fire" (20:14), and "the burning pool of fire and sulphur, which is the second death" (21:8). Commentators have pointed out that the references to hell in the New Testament exhibit apocalyptic imagery that must not be taken literally. For example, in such a context, *eternal* fire may mean long-enduring fire rather than time without end.

The harrowing of hell by Jesus Christ has been a rich source of poetic metaphor. Accordingly, Jesus overcomes the underworld kingdom of sin, evil, and death. He binds Satan in his own house and despoils him of his captives. Dante leaves Satan frozen immobile in ice in the nethermost part of hell.[9] Thus the harrowing of hell sees Jesus raking through the dead for those who do not belong there, who are there only because the gates of heaven were closed until the Savior opened them when he rose to the right hand of the Father. Jesus redeems the souls of the just and leads them from hell. He descends like Orpheus in search of Eurydice, who was beloved. He comes with power; the earth quakes and the tombs burst open in Matthew's account of the redeeming of the dead: "And behold, the veil of the sanctuary was torn in two from top to bottom. The earth quaked, rocks were split, tombs were opened, and the bodies of many saints who had fallen asleep were raised. And coming forth from their tombs after his resurrection, they entered the holy city and appeared to many" (27:51–53).

What this reading of a specific hell says is this: Jesus' victory over death is unconditional; it is total and without obstacle. Jesus dies with everyone, but he also triumphs over everything in earth, in heaven, and in hell. Neither the space below the earth, nor the time forgotten in the past, can escape the Christ-event. Salvation reaches to the ends of the world, to the breadth and length and depth of being itself. Even in Satan's stronghold, the Lord is ever victorious. There remains no place he cannot go; there is no limit to his mercy. Christ risen is truly the consummation of the ages.

Although the creed affirms that Christ dissolved the *limbus patrum*, or "limbo of the fathers" who died in the faith, there was less confidence that Jesus had dissolved the limbo of unbelievers and of children who died before the age of reason. Without faith, it was argued, one could not be saved. Whereas there might be an implicit faith in an adult, what could be said for the child who dies prematurely? An ecclesiology that makes circumcision necessary for salvation, or baptism in the church, or faith in Christ known by name, or the age of reason, excludes from the Kingdom of God more than half of the human race. A more generous ecclesiology allows for baptism of desire and for the mercy of God to work with everyone in ways and places that we know not of. "Neither are your ways my ways," says the Lord (Is. 55:8). At the foot of the cross two thieves were crucified with Jesus, one was penitent and the other was not. To tie God's hands in the case of sinners, unbelievers, or underage children would seem to pretend to know the ways of God and to limit the resourcefulness of the Almighty who wills to save everyone. From an eternal point of view, where yesterday and tomorrow are but a moment, hope in the mercy of God is well founded in the infinite resourcefulness of the saving intent of the Almighty Father. In the phrase, "descended into hell," the creed wishes to affirm reasons for hope.

The story of the fallen angels, which has but a weak reference in the Bible, mostly in Revelation, has led the imagination to conclude that the warfare of humankind and God would be a costly war, with many casualties, and with a victory by God over a decimated humanity. To lose "souls," however, casts no credit on God's infinite wisdom, power, and love. A good school is judged not by the number of students it dismisses, but by the large number that it saves from failure. In the Book of Jonah, the prophet preaches to the metropolis of Nineveh; it took three days to walk across the city which was large enough to stand for the world. To the prophet's surprise and even disappointment, everyone is converted. From the King down to the domestic animals, every single being does penance. We need that kind of hope.

The doctrine of the "descent into hell" wishes finally to say that God is sovereign even in hell, even in the underworld and the afterdeath. There are no off limits to God, and there is no kingdom of evil that operates in opposition to his sovereign will. With what attitude then do we read the creed? Is there a hell to fear? Most of what we imagine about hell comes to us from the imagination of John Milton and Dante Alighieri, by way of the apocalyptic metaphorical language of the Gospels and the Book of Revelation in their image-laden references to hell. The Gospels indeed do say there is a hell, and no one should wish to pull the teeth of these texts, sometimes phrases

in the words of Jesus. Philosophy would argue in a supportive way
that if there can be a free and genuine "yes" given to God by the life
choices of someone in this world, it has to be possible to say "no"
to God. Neither scripture nor philosophy know if there are many people in hell, if any one person, however wicked in our eyes, is in hell,
or for that matter if anyone is in hell. That hell exists we believe.
That an eternal "no" to God is possible we believe. Beyond that we
do not know.

The essence of hell is the absence of God. We also think that
human beings perdure body and soul. In the life after death they remain somehow body and soul. We believe in "the resurrection of the
body." Thus the body will share in the loss of God. However, hell as
the vengeful torture of an angry God speaks more of human hate than
divine justice. Justice does seem to demand that there be some difference in the lot after death of those who led good lives at great cost
and those who led wicked lives on this earth. The doctrine of purgatory tries to take that sense of justice into account in some way. Nonetheless, if people become irredeemably evil, they would seem more
fit for hell than purgatory. But, much remains that we do not know.
We do know that God is infinitely resourceful, that God wills to save
us all. We do know that God is sovereignly wise, powerful, and good,
and that God's grace works within our freedom without taking away
its integrity. Commonsense fear of hell is not unreasonable, but anx-
ious and despairing fear shows little faith and hope. When Joan of Arc
at her trial was asked whether she was confident of being in the state
of grace that led to salvation, she wisely responded: "If I am not, may
God bring me to it; if I am, may God keep me in it."[10] Such is Christian hope.

To escape such a loving and resourceful God would seem more
difficult than to say "yes" to God. The spouse who can bring his or
her partner to do what he or she wishes has learned how to be intui-
tive and diplomatic. The successful spouse has known how to suggest something, how to make an idea appear as the other person's own
idea, when to bring it up, how to propose it, and how to appeal to
motivation. But human spouses, however adroit, are only human and
their resourcefulness is limited. With God we deal with someone of
infinite resourcefulness, who knows us and our minds and hearts from
the inside out, for God made our freedom, sustains, and holds us in
the palm of God's hand. "'Behold, I have graven you on the palms of
my hand,' says the Lord" (Is. 49:16).

Purgatory as a place, a "third place" beside heaven and hell, seems to have been a development of twelfth-century theology.[11] Previously, there had been a doctrine of purgative fire, a divine fire that cleanses and renews like the mythological holocaust of the Phoenix that rises reborn out of its own ashes. The sense of the divine fire had scriptural roots in Paul, who speaks of "the fire [itself] will test the quality of each one's work" (1 Cor. 3:13) and "But if someone's work is burned up, that one will suffer loss; the person will be saved, but only as through fire" (1 Cor. 3:15). In Matthew, John the Baptist speaks of Jesus: "He will baptize you with the holy Spirit and fire" (3:11). Medieval life knew the transformative power of the blacksmith's forge and the baker's oven; it called upon divine justice through the presumptive practice of "trial by fire," by which the innocent were thought to be unharmed by the flames of this earth.

Dante's *Divine Comedy* places "Purgatorio" as ante-chamber to heaven, rather than as a demi-hell. In such a theology, purgatory is a place of certain hope, a place of communion and reciprocal love among the saints, a second chance for sanctity, a nuanced justice that distinguished between the damned and the saved, who were nonetheless sinful and in need of purification. Such a middle place followed upon a theology of a middle sin (venial sin) and created something of a middle class, those who were too good for hell and not good enough yet for heaven.

Purgatory in its best understanding was not just a demi-hell where the dead go after this world's time has passed them, but rather as the waiting room of heaven where the work of grace continued somehow. It was the border where communion between time and eternity, between the living and the dead, between the historical world and the eschatological world of God transpired. Not wholly physical, nor wholly spiritual, Purgatory was seen as the transition from this life to the next, a transition that was an intimate part of the "communion of saints." A materialistic understanding and approach to prayers and indulgences for the dead on the part of the living led to a debilitation of the doctrine of Purgatory at the time of the Protestant Reformation. The eclipse of the doctrine of Purgatory followed upon its exaggeration. The contemporary change in the translation of the creed from "the descent into hell" to "the descent to the dead" may indicate a similar reassessment of the exaggerated emphasis placed on the fiery and vengeful doctrine of hell. Richard McBrien points out that the word *hell* is nowhere mentioned in the documents of Vatican II nor in Paul VI's "Credo of the People of God."[12]

EPILOGUE

Lord of the Absurd

In the fifth article the creed declares that Jesus is Lord even of hell, Lord over even what is dead, Lord of whatever may seemingly be opposed to God, Lord even of non-being and apparent nothingness. There is no further down than hell, no darker yet, no worse oblivion to be searched out. Jesus, Son of God made human, descends to the bottom of the universe, to the farthest point from God, to the darkest night, where the light of even God might seem too distant to penetrate. Into that abyss of past generations gone and seemingly wasted comes the Lord of the absurd. There is no being that can escape God, no fear, fate, or force to overthrow God. Jesus is Lord of hell as well as heaven.

What is said about us follows. Death, burial, and the underworld are not the end of human beings. To descend to hell and yet return to life is not just a fiction of our heart's desire. The hellishness of this world of Holocaust and Hiroshima does not outrun the providence of God. There is no "hell," in hell or on earth, that can escape the victorious presence of Jesus who suffered, was crucified, was dead, was buried, and descended into hell. Nor have the people numberless, whose graves sprinkle our countryside with their earthly remains, been abandoned to perish utterly. They have been included in the death and resurrection of Jesus Christ. Those in hell were the first fruits of the restoration of the Many destined to be at one with the One God.

ARTICLE VI

To TURN TO THE sixth article: "On the third day he rose again."
The immediate insight sees the immortality of Jesus who returns to
life, now to die no more. Death is overcome. Life prevails in God. The
tomb is empty, and the heavy rock of death pushed back.

The further insight recognizes a temptation to view the empty
tomb as a proof of the resurrection, and the appearances of Jesus as
his return to this world. The resurrection is more than reanimation,
and eternal life is more than endless life as we know it. Resurrection
is utter transfiguration; it is new life. The risen Jesus remains a far
greater mystery than the miracle of an empty tomb or the appearance
of a Jesus brought back to this life. The resurrection presents Jesus
born anew to eternal life. His wounds are glorious, and his transfigured body surpasses all the beauty of this world.

Tertia Die Resurrexit a Mortuis

The Latin "tertia die resurrexit a mortuis" means "on the third day he rose [again] from the dead." The resurrection is juxtaposed with the descent into hell. The Easter event centers the sweep of Jesus' triumph over death, from the descent into hell to the ascent into heaven (in the next article). At the bottom of the journey to the underworld, the nadir of the earth and the end of the past, one can imagine that Jesus begins the ascent to the upperworld which will culminate in his ascent to the zenith of the heavens and the end of the future.

The "third day" appears as a calendar detail, according to the scriptures. In the Gospel accounts the tomb is discovered empty early on the morning of the first day of the week. Since Jesus was crucified in all likelihood before the eve of the Sabbath, the *third day* in the creed would seem a shorthand reference to Easter Sunday. Friday, the day of crucifixion, was the first day, which ended with the burial before sunset. Saturday was the second day which began at sunset on Friday. Sunday is thus the third day, and between dawn and sunrise the women discover the empty tomb. An assumption may arise in the reader's mind that Jesus rose just prior to the women's discovery of the empty tomb. Such a time scenario is not demanded by the tombside narratives. When Jesus rose is never given. No one witnesses the actual resurrection event; the women and the apostles discover only the empty tomb. They are told by angels that Jesus is risen.[1] In the Gospel of John, Jesus does predict that he will rise on the third day: "Destroy this temple and in three days I will raise it up" (2:19). It is hard to know, however, whether this information is an editorial insertion after the fact of Easter, or whether these words represent a direct and prophetic quotation from Jesus himself about his future.

In the Old Testament, "three days" was a sacred interval, a time of anticipation sufficient to show forth God's hand in glory. Hosea, for example, writes: "After two days he [the Lord] will revive us; on the third day he will raise us up, that we may live before him" (6:2). Athanasius argues that Jesus was required to delay the resurrection a decent interval in order that his death might be grieved as an actual event;[2] however, the interval could not be too long lest death seem to be victorious. In short, long enough to be dead; not long enough to be abandoned. Martha in the Gospel tells Jesus at the tomb of Lazarus: "Lord, by now there will be a stench; he has been dead for four days" (John 11:39). Perhaps the third day was the limit that the body could be expected to forestall the ravages of death. Surely the "third day" proclaims that Jesus truly died.

The "third day" also provides the story time for the "descent into hell." The idle Sabbath invites an imaginative elaboration of the "descent into hell." Notice, however, that this very anthropomorphic narrative of the resurrection in terms of our space and time coordinates already implies that Jesus overcame death long before Easter morning. It is indeed the risen Jesus who harrows hell. Any description of the resurrection event runs into the difficulty of describing in earthly metaphor the reality of an event in God's eternity beyond historical measurement. Jesus did not rise to a space-time world as we know it, but we can narrate the resurrection only in terms of our experience here and now.

In the earliest written account of the resurrection, Paul writes that Jesus "was raised on the third day in accordance with the scriptures" (1 Cor. 15:4). Paul's language might suggest Jesus was *raised* (passive voice) by the power of God. The creedal language suggests, however, that Jesus rose by his own power as Lord, for the Latin *resurrexit* is active voice. Perhaps Paul sees the resurrection from the perspective of the humanity of Jesus, and the creed sees it from the perspective of the divinity.

Following the text in Paul above, the Nicene Creed adds "according to the scriptures" (1 Cor. 15:4). One thinks also of the risen but unrecognized Jesus walking on the road to Emmaus with two of his disciples, explaining to them the Old Testament scriptures of how the Messiah must suffer in order to enter into his kingdom (Luke 24). The "suffering servant" passages of Isaiah also come to mind readily.

Paul's testimony about the resurrection contains little description. In fact, he gives no account of the empty tomb. He proclaims that the Easter event is crucial and decisive, and witnessed by many believers. For Paul, the resurrection is the keystone of salvation history, binding the world into an enormous arch. Time "Before Christ" is wed to time after Christ "Anno Domini." B.C. and A.D. comprise all of history, with Jesus in his earthly life the keystone at the apex of the arch of time. Pull out the keystone, cast doubt upon the resurrection, and the whole span of salvation history collapses into a delusion. "If for this life only we have hoped in Christ, we are the most pitiable people of all" (1 Cor. 15:19).

That many people came to believe in the resurrection, and that their lives overcame the fear of death that cramps all our virtues, seemed to many observers a kind of proof of the resurrection taken from the witness of resurrected lives. One might infer the cause from the effects. One might also conclude that the effects will only gradually permeate all times and places, all nations and peoples. Thus, the war with death has been won with Christ's victory, although battles here and there may continue for a time. The rain flood has ceased with the resurrection of Jesus, though the flood waters may only gradually subside. When the light has appeared to our eyes, the sun is risen, although it may take time for its warmth to renew the face of the earth. The hook is set, but one must play out the line to catch the fish of this world. Christ is risen, but we wait for the fullness of grace in our mortal bodies. Paul writes: "We know that all creation is groaning in labor pains even until now; and not only that, but we ourselves, who have the firstfruits of the Spirit, we also groan within ourselves as we wait for adoption, the redemption of our bodies" (Rom. 8:22–23).

In the customary English translation, the word "again" appears, despite no indication of it in the Latin. "On the third day he rose *again* from the dead." The use of "again" to mean restoration to a former state has become obsolete in English today.[3] We might still, however, say something like this: "It is time to turn again and go home." We mean it is time to turn back home. We still say "gainsay" (again-say), which means to answer back or argue in the opposite way. Thus to rise again is to rise back from the dead. Jesus rises back from the dead, but since the dead dwell in the underworld, the first "appearance" of the risen Jesus is to the dead. On the third day he rises again, for the living, who encounter him Easter Sunday.

Neither in Paul nor in the Gospels is there any eyewitness account of the resurrection itself. The apocryphal Gospel of Peter contains an eyewitness account, but the faith community did not embrace it as an acceptable witness. We do not know the how of the resurrection. We may not even know when and where it happened. When and where may even be the wrong questions to ask of an event that transcends our world. The Gospels do indeed give accounts of the discovery of the empty tomb on Sunday morning, and the Gospels also narrate several resurrection appearances of Jesus, as we will see below.

The discovery of the empty tomb on the third day does not in and of itself prove that Jesus rose from the dead, but only that something unaccountable transpired, which might be either marvelous or sinister. The body may have been moved, or stolen, by any number of people for any number of reasons. In this regard, Christians believe in the witness of the empty tomb, but do not claim it alone as the proof of anything. A non-empty tomb, however, while not utterly irreconcilable with resurrection faith in the minds of some Christians, would quite likely create a problem of credibility for the disciples who, unlike us, could visit the tomb in order to ponder the meaning of the later appearances. They may well have suffered doubt beyond remedy had the tomb not been empty. We are less affected by the empty tomb witness. Long after the time of Christ, Christians still believe in their own bodily resurrection, but not necessarily that their identical molecular body, put into the ground, will be gathered up again, regardless of the dissolution of centuries.

Faith in Jesus alive was generated by his appearances to his disciples, which appearances were very personalized. Mary Magdalene heard her name spoken by Jesus; Thomas had to be given access to probe the wounds of the Lord, though he does not actually touch Jesus. The Emmaus disciples recognize Jesus in the breaking of the bread; the disciples fishing recognize him in the cooking of breakfast for them on the shore in the dawn's early light. In the experience of these appearances, the empty tomb became a sign of the resurrection, while the discovery of the empty tomb also prepared the disciples for the appearances of Jesus.[4] Nonetheless, the appearances are not proofs, not a second earthly incarnation. Their somewhat elaborate narration in Luke and John would seem to indicate editorial reflection at a later date in the composition of the resurrection accounts.

Throughout the Gospel appearances Jesus is described as somehow more than a resuscitated Lazarus, whom Jesus raised from the dead (John 11) and who will die again, and somehow less than a heavenly spirit who remains aloof from this world. Jesus is not limited by time and space, and yet he is not separated from them either. He appears in the midst of the disciples with the doors being shut. He disappears after the "breaking of the bread." They do come to recognize their friend and Lord, the man they knew from Nazareth. Jesus even carries the wounds of the crucifixion, the particular scars of his earthly life that provide the historical fingerprints of his particular body, now risen from the dead. Moreover, Jesus can be seen, but not immediately nor necessarily recognized. Had he appeared to the eyes of his enemies and unbelievers, they would not have known him. Besides the sight of Jesus, the faithful disciple needed to be given insight. Those who already believed in Jesus of Nazareth were those most likely to believe in the risen Lord.

The Gospels give an account of the resurrection, but not entirely an historical one. The four evangelists give witness to the faith of the Christian community in the resurrection. They do not give an apologetic demonstration. Theirs is the testimony of faith of the early church, whose very existence and dramatic growth might make some sort of reasonable claim for the attention of the skeptic. In the creed it is clear that we *believe* in Jesus Christ our Lord, who was born, died, rose, and will come again. Had one placed a videotape recorder outside the tomb, it may have recorded nothing to play back, not because no actual event took place, but because the resurrection is not an historical event designed for such observation. Rather the resurrection is a trans-historical mystery of God, beyond time and space, yet somehow not apart from it. One thinks again of the mystery of the One and the Many. The resurrection provides for a faith and love that unites human beings to the infinite and sovereign Lord of the universe.

This intersection of time and eternity defies description and explanation. The mystery of the infinite One and the created Many has a similar intersection in the beginning of time. Classical theology calls it creation from nothing. The created Many also begs a future from the infinite God. That hope begins with the Covenant, such as the Old Testament promises to Abraham, to Moses, and to David. They believed somehow that the dance would go on; they believed the Kingdom of God without end would come, where humankind in relationship with God would perdure. All of this is adumbrated in the first article of the creed: "I believe in God the Father Almighty." In the second article of the creed and the following six articles that unfold it, we are given the definitive intersection of God and humanity. Eternity and time meet in Jesus; the One and the Many are demonstrated. Jesus is the Word of God made flesh in a union ever irrevocable. He is the new creation, the new and everlasting covenant. Generations of humanity beg a future from the Father of Our Lord Jesus Christ. The resurrection of the man Jesus to sit at the right hand of the Father gives a pledge that the dance goes on. The Kingdom of God has come, and that Kingdom will be fulfilled in the final coming of this same Jesus who was taken up into the heavens and who sent the Holy Spirit as the promised Comforter, until that day when Christ will be all in all, ever giving over the Kingdom to his Father.

EPILOGUE

Lord of Life

In the sixth article the creed declares the victory of life over death in the resurrection of Jesus from the dead. God is Lord of life. Even if death is an unavoidable part of life, it does not have the last word. Death dies; life lives. The Lord of life has risen. The moment of suspense has passed. He rose on the third day, now no more to die.

For us what follows is this. If we die with Jesus Christ in his faith in the lordship of the Father, we shall rise with him and know with him that God is Lord of life over death. That we all shall live forever is the only concern worthy of serious hope. If we lose that outcome, we have lost everything. If we live, we have found our way to God. The Many, vulnerable in its creaturehood and seemingly put outside of God, here discovers that it belongs in Christ to the One in life everlasting.

ARTICLE VII

To TURN TO THE seventh article: "He ascended into heaven, and is seated at the right hand of the Father." The immediate insight sees the exaltation of Jesus in the ascension into heaven. The levitation and enthronement of Jesus completes and celebrates the resurrection. Jesus, a human being like us, enters heaven and takes his place at the side of God in glory.

The further insight sees the ascension as a revelation of the sovereignty of God. The session, or sitting at the right hand, signifies the consummate governance of the universe. On-going providence, which molds all things gently but comprehensively, now lies in human hands. The lyric, "He's got the whole world in his hands," does not exaggerate. These are the same hands pierced with nails for love of us. The pantocrator Father-Almighty and the seated Jesus Christ are but one sovereign God, King of kings and Lord of lords.

Ascendit ad Coelos

The Latin "ascendit ad coelos," means "he ascended into the heavens." The same plural form of heaven is used in this article as in the phrase "creator of heaven and earth." In English we prefer the singular. Thus "he ascended into heaven" remains the customary translation. Just as Jesus descended into the depths of hell, so now he ascends into the heights of heaven. Just as he was emptied of his glory to be born in Bethlehem stable, so now Jesus is exalted to God's glory in the enthronement at the Father's right hand. The Christ-event, therefore, spans low and high, past and future. The Son of God could be compared to the sun in high heaven, of which the Psalmist says: "Its rising is from the end of the heavens, and its circuit to the end of them; and there is nothing hid from its heat" (19:6). The ascension closes the circle of God's comprehensive providence and salvation in the world that God created; nothing can escape God's embrace.

Liturgically, the church celebrates the ascension forty days after Easter. After a further prayer period of ten days the liturgy celebrates the coming of the Holy Spirit at pentecost. Theologically, one might speak of the Christ-event as one mystery with four aspects: the descent into hell, the resurrection, the ascension, and the descent of the Holy Spirit. It is understandable that the church community would want sufficient time to celebrate each aspect of this tremendous mystery and to linger leisurely over the meaning of these momentous events, just as Mary "kept all these things, reflecting on them in her heart" (Luke 2:19).

The space-time coordinate of the ascension, however, offers us the same difficulty as the descent into hell. Does "descent" and "ascent" reflect merely the cosmography of the ancient world or something more? How much is metaphor and how much is history? Are we dealing in the creed with the levitation of Jesus or only his exaltation portrayed in an elaborate imagery? Heaven is not a place as we know place; heaven transcends the time-space parameters of this world. To ask where is heaven, or to judge heaven is *up* because we so imagine it, would seem to confuse time and eternity. Similarly, to fix on the calendar the ascension at a given moment after the Easter appearances, because we so imagine the "assumption" of his earthly body into heaven at a given time and place, would seem also to confuse time and eternity.

In the Gospels, only Luke talks of the ascension. In his resurrection account, the empty tomb is discovered in the eastern dawn. Jesus then appears to his disciples during the day, and ascends into heaven in the evening of that same first day of the week: "Then he led them [out] as far as Bethany, raised his hands, and blessed them. As he blessed them he parted from them and was taken up to heaven" (Luke 24: 50–51). In Luke's Acts, however, Jesus ascends some weeks later, "appearing to them during forty days, and speaking about the kingdom of God" (1:3). Just as Jesus was hungry and tempted for forty days, so he appears in glorified body for forty days. It is not, however, likely that the "forty" reflects an historical number as much as it does a sacred number. For forty years the Israelites wandered in the desert; for forty days and nights Moses fasted on the mountain of God; for forty days and nights the rains fell in the Deluge. In Luke's Gospel account, Jesus ascends from Bethany; in Acts, the ascent takes place from the nearby site of the Mount of Olives. Where once Jesus had been sorrowful unto death in his agony in the garden, now he is exalted and raised to the bosom of the Father. Just as with the account of the resurrection we speak of an event beyond camera and tape recorder, so in the ascension we transcend the descriptive details of time and space in this world.

Jesus ascends into the *heavens*. These are the same "heavens" that God is creator of, and the ascension has overtones of a homecoming. From ancient times the mountain top was considered to be close to God, because God dwelt above where the sky was immense and matter was evanescent. The spirit-god and the sky-god dominate the pantheon. The imagery in the creed picks up this blue sky that is the home of God, or as the Hebrew scripture would say, the "footstool" of God. Enoch and Elijah are carried up bodily into the heavens as the place of God. Moses talks to God on the top of Mount Horeb, and Jesus is transfigured before his disciples on top of Mount Tabor, his face shining like the sun.

Nonetheless, the return of Jesus to heaven signifies something more than a return to a created heaven. Jesus ascends to the uncreated heaven that is intimacy and accessibility to God due the rightful and only begotten Son of God. As adopted sons and daughters we too will be invited into intimacy with God according to our capacity as creatures of God. One commentator points out the practice in icon painting of making the sky not blue but gold in color, to signify that man's life must be seen not against a cosmological background but against a theological one where God is the eternal bright origin and end of our existence.[1] Gold is incorruptible; gold is treasureful. This relatedness to God that is human destiny remains a golden vocation. Emerson once said: "Man is a golden impossibility." While that may be true in this world, it is not true in the fullness of salvation, when we will ascend to dwell where Jesus sits in the Kingdom of God. There the light never fails and the sky is always golden. Jesus' ascent into heaven proclaims his return into the depths of God's being.

If we prescind from the narrative theology of the resurrection and ascension, we might speak simply of the exaltation and glorification of Jesus as a single movement without separation or division. Not that one must conclude that the resurrection-and-ascension took place at the instant of death on the cross. To so conclude would be to return again into a narrative theology time-frame, and a theology probably less rich than Luke's. The ascension is rather a way of expressing the fullness of the resurrection. Because Jesus was finally and fully exalted, we know more how to appreciate the empty tomb together with the earthly appearances of Jesus. The appearances gave credence to the empty tomb, and the ascension gives amplification to the appearances. Truly the Lord is risen. The ascension thus mediates between the resurrection from the tomb and the fulsome glorification of the Son of Man at the right hand of the Father. The ascension suggests how one event leads to the other, or more exactly, how the one event is the other. To die, to rise from the dead, to ascend into heaven, and to sit at the Father's side, comprise the one Paschal Mystery broken into facets for our contemplation.

Jesus tells Mary Magdalene in the resurrection garden: "Stop holding onto me, for I have not yet ascended to the Father. But go to my brothers and tell them, 'I am going to my Father and your Father, to my God and your God'" (John 20:17). The appearance of Jesus to Mary did not mean the return of Jesus as of old. This Jesus cannot be held down to one time and one place. This Jesus fills all times and places; the Spirit of Jesus blows everywhere like the wind. The Christ-event is not once, but then and also now. Just as creation must be sustained and the almightiness of God continues to uphold all that exists, so the Paschal Mystery is a sustaining event, celebrated in sacrament, known in human experience. Jesus is now always with us, not so much as an outsider, but rather because we are incorporated in him. In this way only can Mary Magdalene hold on to the Lord.

Jesus told the disciples that it was good for them that he depart, because then he would send the Spirit to remind them of all he had told them. Furthermore, he goes "to prepare a place" for them, so that where he is they may also be. In short, Jesus has not so much gone from us as taken us with him to God. In the Lucan ascension in Acts the disciples stand looking into heaven. They are paralyzed with indecision or grief, when "two men stood by them in white robes, and said, 'Men of Galilee, why are you standing there looking at the sky? This Jesus who has been taken up from you into heaven will return in the same way as you have seen him going into heaven'" (Acts 1: 10–11). Thus, the ascension tells the church not to drop out of life to await the imminent coming of Jesus in glory, as some believers had predicted, but to run on with history in the strength of the Spirit that Jesus would send into their hearts. Christ lives in them; then get to work. Jesus remains in heaven, and they must be his hands and feet in this world. The grieving over the earthly Jesus must end; new life must go on. For the church, this new life stems from the Spirit; it is life in the real presence of Jesus in the Eucharist; it is life in the patient hope of the final coming, the hour of which only the Father knows.

Sedet ad Dexteram Dei Patris Omnipotentis

The Latin "sedet ad dexteram Dei Patris omnipotentis" means "is seated [sits] at the right [hand] of God the Father almighty." The symbol of power and rank in the position at the right hand of the king would be easily understood in the ancient world. To this day an indispensable colleague is called our "right-hand man." The creedal phrasing comes from the Bible, both New and Old Testament. At the end of the Marcan appendix we read: "So then the Lord Jesus, after he spoke to them, was taken up into heaven and took his seat at the right hand of God. But they went forth and preached everywhere, while the Lord worked with them and confirmed the word through accompanying signs." (Mark 16:19–20). Psalm 110 opens with these lines: "The Lord says to my lord: 'Sit at my right hand, till I make your enemies your footstool.'" The Gospel puts those words on Jesus' lips in controversy with the Scribes over the Christ as the son of David, and yet the lord of David (see Mark 12:35–37). This son of David who is yet David's lord is confessed to be Jesus Christ, and the Gospel may borrow its imagery directly from such passages. Other places in scripture give support for this phrasing: For example, Luke writes of Jesus saying at his trial: "But from this time on the Son of Man will be seated at the right hand of the power of God" (22:69).

The exaltation of Jesus, already confessed "consubstantial with the Father," presents a powerful antidote for the idolatrous claims of an Emperor, such as Augustus, who enjoyed God-like status in the empire when he died. Jesus, who was born under the rule of Augustus and unjustly judged under a Roman procurator, now is exalted above all earthly powers and dominions. Jesus judges the world at the right hand of the Father. This is the apotheosis of the Son of Man. "For everyone who exalts himself will be humbled, and the one who humbles himself will be exalted" (Luke 14:11). Born in a stable, nailed to a cross between two thieves, Jesus now is glorified at the side of God. He is the power beside the throne, the only Son at his Father's right hand.

In this second part of the seventh article of the creed, we are given a glimpse of the heavenly court in sovereign session. Jesus, wed irrevocably to the flesh, is solemnly enthroned. The incarnation was indeed not dissolved after the earthly life of Jesus; his flesh is forever. Humanity, long distant from God, now could not be any closer. Jesus who is Lord receives full sovereignty. *Ecce homo* becomes "behold Christ the King." We use the image of "the seat of justice" for a Supreme Court, or a "chair in philosophy" for authority to teach in a university. Jesus "sits," just as the court that sits or the university that chairs is said to be "in session" (seated). The Lord of history thus sits upon the throne. Helmut Thielicke calls this session "the festival of Jesus' Lordship."[2] John the Evangelist has Jesus enthroned even upon the cross: "So Jesus said [to them], 'When you lift up the Son of Man, then you will realize that I AM, and that I do nothing on my own, but I say only what the Father taught me'" (8:28).

The creed follows the more traditional narrative theology: crucifixion, descent into hell, ascent into heaven, enthronement in the chair of justice, and finally the second coming to judge living and dead. Both the Nicene Creed and the Old Roman Creed, which preceded the established text of the Apostles' Creed, omit the "Dei" (of God) and the "omnipotentis" (of the almighty). Those texts read simply that Jesus sits at the right hand of the Father. In short, the Son returns to the bosom of the Father from whence he came into this world. The fuller text of the Apostles' Creed clearly reflects the first article: "I believe in *God* the Father *Almighty*." We have already seen that the Father, when understood as the Pantocrator-Father, enjoys all the sustaining and governing attributes of *Almighty God*. When "Father" came to be used more specifically for the subsistent relationship of the Father to the Son, the additional wording allowed both meanings of *Father* clearly to emerge.

EPILOGUE

Lord of History

In the seventh article Jesus ascends and sits at the right hand of God. King of kings, he now reigns from on high. The history of the world and all its events ultimately issue from this throne of God, where Jesus in the flesh holds the sovereignty as king of the world. Providence reaches out in on-going power to unfold creation from within, without denigrating the inner nature of matter nor the essence of human freedom. God remains sovereign, but now not the theistic God of the first article, but rather the Son of the Father enfleshed who rules the affairs of humanity.

For us what follows is this. No event in our life just happens. In the last analysis, the events in our life are given by God, yet in and through our own freedom. Our world is not an errant space lab, with God in impotent anguish that what once the Almighty launched cannot now be guided. Consummate resourcefulness and wisdom prevail in human hands, for Jesus sits at the right hand of the Father almighty.

ARTICLE VIII

To TURN TO THE eighth article: "He will come again to judge the living and the dead." The immediate insight sees the second coming as the final judgment. Humankind will be separated into two groups: the one to be rewarded for the good done in this life, the other to receive the punishment that justice requires. The Great Assize at the end of time will finally give justice. Jesus will preside as universal judge beyond any appeal. Each of us will stand before the judgment bench.

The further insight sees the second coming as much a revelation of the triumph of the infinite resourcefulness of the grace of God in this world as a reward or punishment for human initiatives. More than being sentenced, we will recognize ourselves as we have become through grace. More than having justice imposed, we will see revealed the justice all along hidden in our lives and in the world. What had been gradually graced from within will now be disclosed in all its grace filled transfiguration. Jesus will come as the supreme artist who brings to the masterpiece of creation the final touches. Such a coming to judge need not be feared, but longed for and eagerly awaited. Jesus will be Lord in the ending, just as he was in the beginning. Jesus will be like the presider at a wedding, who witnesses the vows of the beloved bride of God. "The Spirit and the bride say, 'Come.' Let the hearer say, 'Come.' Let the one who thirsts come forward, and the one who wants it receive the gift of life-giving water" (Rev. 22:17).

Inde Venturus Est Judicare Vivos et Mortuos

The Latin "inde venturus est judicare vivos et mortuos" means "from there [thence] he will come to judge the living and the dead." Jesus will come (again) to judge the world. "He [Jesus] commissioned us to preach to the people and testify that he is the one appointed by God as judge of the living and the dead" (Acts 10:42). The return of Jesus *then* will manifest that he indeed sits *now* as the judge of the universe. "For the time that has passed is sufficient for doing what the Gentiles like to do . . . but they will give account to him who stands ready to judge the living and the dead" (1 Peter 4:3, 5).

The eighth article of the creed encompasses the future. Jesus once came in Bethlehem of Judaea; he now sits at the right hand of the Father; he *will come* again in glory. The past belongs to God, and the present, and even the future. The creed points to the fulfillment of human history. God's time stretches back to "in the beginning" and confidently awaits the fullness of time "in the end." Creation in time and space had a beginning; it will have an ending just as wonderful, just as full of the wisdom, power, and goodness of the sovereign Father as ever. History will be fulfilled; the work of creation will be completed; his kingdom will come on earth as in heaven in the last days. Initial creation will be consummated in that final creation on the day of the Lord. Eternity will gather time in its embrace, not to dissolve time but to preserve it, to justify it, to overcome its distance from God. The second coming will gather all things into Christ. In Paul's Letter to the Ephesians we read: "In all wisdom and insight he has made known to us the mystery of his will in accord with his favor that he set forth in him as a plan for the fullness of times, to sum up all things in Christ, in heaven and on earth" (1:9–10).

The Greek word for the "second coming" of Jesus is *parousia*. The word captures both the meaning of *presence now* and *coming presence* in the future. It is thus well chosen to reflect the mystery of the *second coming* that we find in this part of the creed. God has already saved the world in the coming of Jesus of Nazareth, and God will save the world in the last coming of Christ in glory. The Kingdom is within you and "now is the acceptable time"; likewise the Kingdom is to come when God in Christ will be all in all. Paul writes:

May the eyes of [your] hearts be enlightened, that you may know
what is the hope that belongs to his call, what are the riches
of glory in his inheritance among the holy ones, and what is the
surpassing greatness of his power for us who believe, in accord
with the exercise of his great might, which he worked in Christ,
raising him from the dead and seating him at his right hand in
the heavens, far above every principality, authority, power, and
dominion, and every name that is named not only in this age
but also in the one to come. And he put all things beneath his
feet and gave him as head over all things to the church, which
is his body, the fullness of the one who fills all things in every
way. (Eph. 1:18–23)

Thus the Christian lives not only by faith, but he or she lives also
by hope.

The end of the world, which coincides with the final coming
of Christ, has been portrayed in scripture and the literature of ancient
times as a day of cataclysmic events and cosmic upheavals. Imaginative literature about the "end times" sounds strange to us, although
our own preoccupation with nuclear holocaust suggests a similar
dread and fascination. Eschatological texts in the New Testament
abound. The end times were thought by many to be imminent. Some
commentators think that Jesus himself, as a man of his time, thought
the end was near. The Gospel records: "'Whoever is ashamed of me
and of my words in this faithless and sinful generation, the Son of
Man will be ashamed of when he comes in his Father's glory with
the holy angels.' He also said to them, 'Amen, I say to you, there are
some standing here who will not taste death until they see that the
kingdom of God has come in power'" (Mark 8:38–9:1). In the ascension narrative in Acts we read: "This Jesus, who has been taken up
from you into heaven, will return in the same way as you have seen
him going into heaven" (1:11). And Paul comments: "For the Lord himself, with a word of command, with the voice of an archangel and
with the trumpet of God, will come down from heaven, and the dead
in Christ will rise first. Then we who are alive, who are left, will be
caught up together with them in the clouds to meet the Lord in the
air. Thus we shall always be with the Lord. Therefore, console one
another with these words" (1 Thess. 4:16–18).

Jesus will come again to *judge*. The sovereign session at the right
hand of the Father will culminate in an apocalyptic assize. Both "session" and "assize" are words related to root words for sitting. It is that

notion of presiding over world history that we should capture with the word "judge." The coming to judge is the fulfillment of sitting at the right hand; the "assize" follows upon the "session." The pantocrator or all-sovereign God who rules all happenings in this world cannot but conclude the outcome of the total sum of human activity. This is the general judgment and the final coming. "Father Almighty" and "Judge of the living and dead" differ only in the direction they face. The former looks to the beginning, the latter to the end.

Men and women, knowing their weakness and sinfulness, tend to fear judgment. Job evaluations produce anxiety in the best of us. What of the evaluation of a lifetime? The life-review that Jesus will come to adjudicate seems in popular imagination to be a bench verdict. Whether it be separation of the sheep on the judge's right from the goats on his left, or some version of individual scrutiny at the supreme bar, the sovereign judge of the living and dead will hold the ultimate "captain's mast." This is summary justice—quick, baldly factual, and without appeal. God is omniscient; nothing remains hidden. The time of mercy is past; now is the righteousness of God seen in reward and punishment. History must not turn out to be mush, with good equivalent to evil, and truth equated with falsehood. No longer will the expediency of Pilate prevail in the way of the world where there is no justice. Silent back then, Jesus will now speak. The Son of Man and Son of God will finally judge with consummate justice. "For the Son of Man will come with his angels in his Father's glory, and then he will repay everyone according to his conduct" (Mt. 16:27).

If "bench judgment" remains our model of judgment, it might be further claimed that no one will receive a sentence that is unfair or even one that they deem unfair. There will be no sour grapes. Everything will be made manifest, and sinners will know their life in its every aspect. "When did we see you hungry and feed you?" (Mt. 25) will be shown in detail. We might well think that such a divine bench judgment would conclude with no regrets, just as with no errors. Accordingly, each person will willingly stand by who and what they are shown to be. They will not need or ask for further length of days to try out alternative ways of life. Here I take my stand at last, they will say. This is indeed the person I wish to be. More revisions and more opportunities will not be wanted; my decision stands. No longer provisional or tentative, my way of life has truly become me. In his novel *Till We Have Faces*, C. S. Lewis argues that at the judgment our masks will all be set aside, and our true face with its few true words will appear;[1] we will receive justly what we always most wanted.

If "bench judgment" promises not only no error, but also no regrets, then the paradigm of the sentencing judge before whom people stand in suspense and fear may not image the judgment of God at all. A no-error and no-regrets judgment appears to be more of a revelation, a disclosure to myself of who I am and what I want. Standing in the full light and truth I come to recognize myself. A story once told me illustrates well judgment as revelation. A young man goes to an evening party, where there is dancing underneath special lighting. Underneath the "black light" in the doorway, it becomes manifest to everyone that the shoulders of his navy blue blazer are covered with shining dandruff, invisible by ordinary light. In dismay, he recognizes his predicament, turns, and runs out of the party in self-rejection and self-condemnation. No one at the party, however, tells him he is unwelcome in his present condition. Rather he judges himself unworthy; he judges that if he were in the place of the other guests he would not be merciful to someone arriving in his own condition. Such a judgment is less a verdict from an authority on high than a recognition of one's own heart. In God's white light, we see ourselves and are judged.

It remains, nonetheless, hard to imagine that anyone would want to be excluded, even with a no-error and no-regrets judgment. Milton has Lucifer say that he would want to be excluded, even with a no-error and no-regrets judgment. Milton's Satan would rather reign in hell than serve in heaven.[2] Fearless angel, apparent conscientious objector, bravely yet sinfully he sets his face against God. Can this be? That a "no" to God remains a genuine possibility would seem a necessary conclusion if an authentic "yes" to God should be possible. That yes-no decision may not involve the name of God; our choice may only involve the overall meaning of our life and the quality of its hope. Dag Hammarskjold's oft-quoted passage in his journal, *Markings*, comes to mind: "I don't know Who—or what—put the question, I don't know when it was put. I don't even remember answering. But at some moment I did answer *Yes* to Someone—or Something—and from that hour I was certain that existence is meaningful and that, therefore, my life in self-surrender, had a goal."[3]

In such a paradigm of judgment, God condemns no one, nor rewards anyone from the outside. Threats after all breed behavior motivated by fear; rewards foster behavior that can easily be meretricious. Accordingly, God sentences no one. God discloses all; God reveals us to ourselves; God appears and "in thy light do we see light" (Ps. 36:9). In an instant we judge ourselves, because we truly see ourselves. If we are loveless, what we are becomes our "punishment." Not to love God is to be in hell. If we are love-full, what we are becomes our "reward." To love God is now to relate to God face to face; such is heaven.

The creed says that Jesus Christ will judge "the living and the dead." English translations until recent times used to render the Latin *vivos* as "quick." Thus, "to judge the quick and the dead." We still speak of being touched to the quick. That whole phrase has been interpreted to mean those alive on earth at the judgment ending of the world, as well as the vast majority of humankind who would by then be numbered among the dead. In a slight shift of meaning, the "living" has been read as the *saved* and the "dead" as the *lost*. More likely, "the living and the dead" refers to time past and time now, all that has been and all that is, everything and everyone from beginning to end.

If the "living and the dead" encompasses everyone and everything in all times and all places, yet another reading of "to judge" emerges. What we confess is that Jesus Christ, our Lord, will also *justify* all things. All of creation will be summed up in humanity and its history. God's justice will appear more in God's activity than in declarations of innocence or guilt. When God judges, things are *made* right. Typewriters that electronically justify the margins might serve as a metaphor. What was a ragged-edged document throughout becomes at the end and in an instant "justified" and adjudged just. So God will justify creation, not just by explaining but by deeds of power that make right. What ought to be, will be. Paul Claudel in his plays speaks of "la belle justice" as that quality of being exactly what God intended. God's word will finally be fulfilled.

Saint Paul uses as a major metaphor for the Christ-event, the term "justification." Paul does not mean primarily that we will be found innocent in a verdict; he wants to speak not so much of what we have done but what God is doing. God's love is reaching out in gratuitous and efficacious grace to make all things new and justify their existence. The coming judgment will justify the ways of God to men. Only at the end of the novel can the author justify the earlier chapters and prove their beauty and fittingness. Only the artist can pass final judgment on the integrity and worth of the artifact. Jesus Christ will justify the ways of God to men finally. He will make just, render judgment, vindicate the entire creation that came from the hand of God the Father all-powerful and ever was subject to God's sovereign providence. In the parable of the wheat and the weeds (Mt. 13:25–39), the husbandman allows the weeds to grow alongside the wheat, lest by prematurely disturbing them while their roots are all entwining, the wheat may be uprooted as well. But at the harvest, the wheat will be separated from the weeds and gathered into the barn. Paul writes of Christian hope that all things will work unto good for them that love God.

> If God is for us, who can be against us? He who did not spare his own Son but handed him over for us all, how will he not also give us everything else along with him? Who will bring a charge against God's chosen ones? It is God who acquits us. Who will condemn? It is Christ [Jesus] who died, rather, was raised, who also is at the right hand of God, who indeed intercedes for us. What will separate us from the love of Christ? Will anguish, or distress, or persecution, or famine, or nakedness, or peril, or the sword? . . . No, in all these things we conquer overwhelmingly through him who loved us. For I am convinced that neither death, nor life, nor angels, nor principalities, nor present things, nor future things, nor powers, nor height, nor depth, nor any other creature will be able to separate us from the love of God in Christ Jesus our Lord. (Rom. 8:31–39)

In the "second coming" micro-events of the individual and macro-events of the human race will stand explained in the dawning light of Christ in the New Jerusalem. "Love is strong as death," says the Song of Songs. Just as death pursues everyone and gains them in the end, so much the more is love pursuing everyone and capturing them in the end. Not only will love prove as resourceful and persevering in the pursuit of its prey as the grim reaper from whom no one escapes, love will prove stronger than death.[4] It will be manifest that God is stronger than all that is non-God. Her grace is prevenient; his grace is efficacious. Our hope in the Kingdom of God is not a hope in humankind, but a hope in the infinitely resourceful God who so loved the world that God sent his only Son.

Just as the origins of creation belong to God, the eighth article of the creed affirms that the future fulfillment of creation belongs to the same Lord. God began the world and God will finish it. God fathers the world with sovereignty, and he will judge (complete and justify) the world with that same fatherly power. If creation is God the Father bringing the world to birth as an infant, the judgment is God the proud father of the bride, bringing the world to the altar. He fathered her; he shall see her happily married.

> Then I saw a new heaven and a new earth. The former heaven
> and the former earth had passed away, and the sea was no more.
> I also saw the holy city, a new Jerusalem, coming down out of
> heaven from God, prepared as a bride adorned for her husband.
> I heard a loud voice from the throne saying, "Behold, God's dwell-
> ing is with the human race. He will dwell with them and they
> will be his people and God himself will always be with them
> [as their God]. He will wipe every tear from their eyes, and there
> shall be no more death or mourning, wailing or pain, [for] the
> old order has passed away. (Rev. 21:1–4)

The pantocrator father of the world is the infinite God seen from the
viewpoint of the beginning of time; the judge of the living and the
dead is the same infinite and sovereign God seen from the viewpoint
of the ending of time. To believe in the Almighty Father in the beginning is to believe in the Almighty Judge at the end. These are two
profiles of the same face of God. And Jesus Christ with human face
will be "judge," that same Jesus who told the parable of the "prodigal
son" and the even more generous *prodigal father.*

In the meantime or "between times" before the final assize, Jesus *sits* at the right hand of the Father, that is to say, he sustains and
governs the creation with the almighty fatherliness of God until the
end. At the end it will be apparent that Jesus Christ was holding session all throughout this interim time. The pantocrator-God judges the
world every moment through the resourceful power of providence;
only at the end, however, will the pantocrator-judge be manifest. As
the Fathers of the church were fond of saying: All things will be recapitulated in Christ. In the apse of the National Shrine of the Im-
maculate Conception in Washington, D.C., there is a seated pan-
tocrator-Christ, sternly posed in a judgmental posture. It is the Lord
of history who is Judge of history. The severity should be read as
power at the ready to justify the world and make the fatherliness of
God bear all of its fruit, rather than a threat to terrify those for whom
God sent God's only Son that the world might be saved through him.
In the judgment it will be seen that Christ is all in all. The love of
the Father is triumphant. "They are accomplished. I [am] the Alpha
and the Omega, the beginning and the end" (Rev. 21:6). Therefore we
confidently say *Maranatha*: "Come, Lord Jesus!" (Rev. 22:20).

The initial Latin word in the eighth article, "inde," is usually
rendered as "thence" or "from there." "Thence" also carries the connotation of time: from then and from there. In earlier creeds the word

unde was often found, but the semantic difference remains minor. "Whence" (from where) is sometimes substituted for "thence" (from there). Both words speak of Jesus coming from the place of the session at the right hand to the assize where the living and the dead are judged. "From there he will come to judge the living and the dead." The reader, however, must not think that "judging" is a species of the generic behavior that constitutes the "sovereign session" of Jesus Christ. The "judging" flows from the fullness of the session; the "judging" is the fulfillment of creation that will consummate the constant sovereign providence of God that the session always represents. All-judging is simply a way of saying full-sessioning, but seen now from the viewpoint of the end of time when the work of the Kingdom of God has been completed.

The Nicene Creed adds that Jesus will come *again* (iterum). The obvious meaning would be that the judgment is a second coming, or a coming again. The Apostles' Creed speaks of Jesus who "rose *again* from the dead." Jesus rose *back* from the dead; he *re-turned* from the dead. The second coming is similar in also being a return. Immemorial would seem to be the human heart's longing for justice at the last. For example, in Homer's *Odyssey,* Penelope and her loyal household await the coming back of Odysseus. If only he would come back, he would right all the injustices now being suffered there. That is the sense of "again" in the Nicene Creed. If only Jesus would come back (again), then all of the injustice of the world would be made right. The Nicene Creed also adds that Jesus will come *in glory* (cum gloria). Paul writes: "When Christ your life appears, then you too will appear with him in glory" (Col. 3:4).

The Nicene Creed concludes with a phrase; "and his kingdom will have no end" (cujus regni non erit finis). It was possible to imagine that the incarnation ended with the cessation of the resurrection appearances of Jesus. If one thought the body of Jesus was but an instrument of the divinity, in order to express itself while in this world, then upon ascending from this world the instrument might seem superfluous. Marcellus of Ancyra had concluded in this vein.[5] The Nicene Creed affirms to the contrary, alluding to the promise of Gabriel to Mary that the Son of the Most High about to be conceived would reign forever: "and he will rule over the house of Jacob forever, and of his kingdom there will be no end" (Luke 1:33). The flesh of Jesus sits at the right hand of God forever. The dance goes on; the covenant is everlasting. The love of God for his Son, which brought the Son to become man, proves to be an irrevocable love. Jesus who is Lord is not provisional; he is not surpassable. He cannot be undone; his reign will never end. In Jesus, God has wed the human race, and eternity has embraced time.

EPILOGUE

Lord of Justice

In the eighth article the creed declares that Jesus is Lord in the ending of the world, just as the Father was Lord in the beginning. Creation was begun from nothing; creation will be fulfilled from everything. As an artist, God will finish the work of creation. God will stand back on that day and say "It is finished" and "It is good." And we will echo how wonderful it is to behold. One thinks of the unfinished figures of Michelangelo's slaves, trapped in their unfinished blocks of marble, yet beheld in the inner eye of the artist. Even now the world of God emerges anew with each further blow of the hammer of time upon the stones. So the world is unfolding as it should, so the world shall be consummated in God. Creation will not turn out disappointing; God's providence will not prove ineffectual. The end will bring justice to what has been and to what should be.

For us what follows is this. While there is no complete justice in this world, there is final justice at the endtime. We are like viewers behind the tapestry that is yet on the loom of time. We see all the loose ends, and the pattern cannot be seen well from the backside. The last thread will be inserted; the last piece of the jigsaw puzzle will reveal the whole picture at last. All will be made manifest. We will see our lives as the contributing threads to God's eternal masterpiece. "Amen! Come, Lord Jesus!"

ARTICLE IX

To TURN TO THE ninth article: "I believe in the Holy Spirit." The immediate insight sees the Spirit as the unseen guest in the human soul that at baptism receives the gift of the Holy Spirit. The many gifts of the Spirit elevate the life of the Christian. Joy, peace, patience, etc., are fruits of the Spirit who works within our activity.

The further insight sees the Holy Spirit as more than the gifts of God. As with the Son of God made human, we encounter the very self-gift of God. Such an infinite treasure also cascades into a cornucopia of visible gifts and fruits. Without the Holy Spirit we do not know how to receive the gift of God. God gives the reception of God's self-gift, which is the Holy Spirit. That Holy Spirit is both gift and its reception. God would not have us miss receiving his great gift, so God sends the Spirit into our hearts. "We have not received the spirit of the world but the Spirit that is from God, so that we may understand the things freely given us by God" (1 Cor. 2:12). More than a panoply of humanistic virtues, the Holy Spirit bestows the theological virtues of faith, hope, and love. These works of the Spirit put us in touch with God's self as gift, and not just with enhanced behavior in this world.

Credo in Spiritum Sanctum

The Latin "Credo in Spiritum Sanctum" means "I believe in the Holy Spirit." The third part of the creed begins with a repetition of the *credo*. The Trinitarian structure that the creed quite early assumed is made more evident thereby. If the first part of the creed speaks of the sovereign Father, and the second part of the Son of God made flesh, then the third part speaks of humankind in communion with the Father who is revealed by the Son, who in turn is confessed Lord by the power of the Holy Spirit of God. "Therefore I tell you that nobody speaking by the Spirit of God says, 'Jesus be accursed!' And no one can say, 'Jesus is Lord,' except by the holy Spirit" (1 Cor. 12:3). The third part of the creed will display the *gesta Spiriti*, just as the second part displayed the *gesta Christi*. These "deeds of the Spirit" are accomplished in the church and speak of the effects of the Christ-event upon humankind.

We are not told about the Holy Spirit primarily in order to satisfy our interest in the metaphysical nature of God; we are told of the Spirit because the presence of the Spirit in our lives gives us crucial understanding about ourselves and our world. We will henceforth be told a story of God within us, just as we were told the story of Jesus Christ among us. We will be told the story of the people of God, the church, in a narrative theology much like the Christological narrative, although less singular. We will be told of the "resurrection of the body" rather than of "on the third day he rose again," and of "the forgiveness of sins" rather than of "he was crucified, was dead, and was buried." Just as articles three through eight brought us finally back to article two, "Jesus is Lord" now understood in all its ramifications, so articles ten through twelve will bring us back to article nine, "the Holy Spirit" now understood in its implications for us men and women today and forever.

Only if one has experienced life as a gift and not an unappreciated "given," can one understand what Christians mean by the Father. Only if one has known in life how death can be transcended, can one understand what Christians mean by Jesus is risen. Only if one has experienced faith and hope and love in one's own life that exceed any of the antecedents that might have explained them, can one understand the Holy Spirit. Theology remains always a reflection upon a prior experience of God. The Holy Spirit is active in the lives of people everywhere; they do indeed experience an inexplicable change of heart, a gift of courage or generosity that is boundless and comes from seemingly nowhere. Most often they do not know whom to thank or how to describe what has happened to them, and what will happen again in the many moments of grace that make up their life before God. The creed offers a quasi-narrative account of the grace of Christ Jesus, because of whom "the love of God been poured out into our hearts through the holy Spirit that has been given to us" (Rom. 5:5).

God has long been described as "spirit," a bodiless entity that is like the wind that blows from where we know not and remains invisible yet full of hidden power to sail ships or uproot trees. John writes: "The wind blows where it wills, and you can hear the sound it makes, but you do not know where it comes from or where it goes; so it is with everyone who is born of the Spirit" (3:8). The Hebrew word for the spirit is *ruah*, which means "breath" or "wind." We cannot live unless we breathe the wind in and out of our bodies. The wind cannot be seen any more than the spirit of God, but without air we are dead. It is everywhere and upon it we are always totally dependent. God breathed spirit into Adam made from clay, and he was given the breath of life. When Jesus dies on the cross, he breathed forth his last and thus "gave up his spirit." The "God bless you" that we say after someone sneezes contains a prayer for their life, lest they lose their breath without recovery and so die. The Greeks call the spirit *pneuma*, and in English we speak of pneumatic pressure. The Romans call the spirit *spiritus*, and in English we speak of vital persons being spirited or lively. Germanic languages call the spirit *geist*, and in English we speak of the Holy Ghost. In popular imagination, of course, ghosts are *bodiless* spirits.

The spirit gives life. The spirit is the soul of the body, the seat of unity and source of all vitality. Just as the Father-almighty was first understood as God-father-source of all being, and only subsequently as the Father of our Lord Jesus Christ, so the Holy Spirit was first understood as the sacred presence and power of God in the world. In the Psalms we read: "When thou sendest forth thy Spirit, they are created; and thou renewest the face of the ground" (104:30). In short, the spirit constitutes the soul of the world. Moreover, in the creedal context, the Holy Spirit is the soul of the body of the human community which is the holy church. In the liturgy we pray: "Come Holy Spirit, and fill the hearts of your faithful and enkindle in them the fire of your love. Send forth your spirit and they shall be created and you will renew the face of the earth." Subsequently the Holy Spirit was understood as the Spirit "who proceeds from the Father [and the Son]."

The re-creation of the world becomes the particular work attributed to the Holy Spirit, the third person of the Blessed Trinity, although this new creation remains the work of the grace of the only Son of the Father, given through the Spirit.

In the classical theology of the Trinity, the Holy Spirit is imaged as the Love between the Father and the Son. Just as the Son of God is the Word of God, so the Holy Spirit is the Love of God. The analogy is drawn from the knowing and loving that is constitutive of human nature, and its formulation was fostered largely by St. Augustine. It remains only an analogy and not an essential explanation of the infinite mystery of God who is origin of knowing and loving. Accordingly, the Father knows the Son, and the love that proceeds from their perfect knowing and being known is the Holy Spirit, who "together with the Father and the Son is adored and glorified." Just as the Word of God took flesh in Jesus, in an analogous way the love of God takes up indwelling in the church, the mystical body of the risen Christ, filled with the Holy Spirit.

The descent of the Holy Spirit upon the apostles dominates the opening of the Acts of the Apostles. In the upper room where they were all gathered in prayer, tongues of fire appear above their heads in a baptism of the Spirit. The sound of a mighty wind, the very breath of God, is heard. The apostles go forth co-missioned to preach, in the tongues of Pentecost, of Jesus who is risen. "Exalted at the right hand of God, he received the promise of the holy Spirit from the Father and poured it forth as you [both] see and hear" (Acts 2:33). The language of the Spirit overcomes all language barriers, because it speaks the universal tongue of the heart of humanity, now not in search of God as the builders of the tower of Babel who proceeded on their own ego-driven initiative, but now in reception of the grace of God through Jesus Christ. Humankind cannot coerce the kingdom of God; humankind must receive the gift of the Spirit. John's baptism came with a cleansing water and repentance; this baptism rushes in with a fire that gives birth again to a new creation, which is the love of God dwelling in our hearts. Pentecost is thus the birth of the church. In a similar way, the Spirit hovered over Mary and she was filled with the Holy Spirit and the Word became flesh. Aquinas says the Spirit is to the church as the soul is to the body.[1] The Spirit gives life, just as the breath of God enlivened the first Adam. So the church members are born out of the baptismal font by the breath of the Spirit who enlivens them unto life everlasting.

The creed follows the narrative theology of the Synoptic Gospels. John's Gospel uses another chronology and a more mystical theology. In the fourth Gospel the church is born on Calvary from the spear-pierced side of Christ, from whence flowed water and blood, the signs of physical birth and the symbols of rebirth that are baptism and the sacrificial love of the Eucharist. Here is the birth of the church when time and eternity intersect; here is the compression of resurrection, ascension, and descent of the Spirit taken out of the time-space frame of the fifty days after Easter. In John, the Christ-event is now placed in the eternal moment of love and surrender when Jesus died and the Father would not let him fall out of his embrace as the beloved Son. Jesus is exalted when he is lifted up on the cross, just as when he ascends to the right hand of the Father in Luke's account. The second coming of Jesus entails the reception of the Holy Spirit now, the spirit of Jesus in every time and place, anticipating the end-of-the-world future coming on the clouds amid glory.

The Nicene Creed adds several clauses to the simple affirmation of the Apostles' Creed, "I believe in the Holy Spirit." These additions were not added at the Council of Nicaea (325), which concluded with a simple declaration of faith in the Spirit. They were added at the Council of Constantinople (381), where disagreement over the role of the Holy Spirit surfaced in church council. The Niceno-Constantinopolitan Creed contains a series of clauses describing the role of the Spirit in much the same way as Nicaea had added qualifying phrases to the second article confessing Jesus as Lord.[2]

Some commentators note that the Nicene Creed begins with the disjunctive *"And* I believe in the Holy Spirit." The *Kai* in Greek may imply from the start that the Holy Spirit remains separate from the Father and the Son in some way. "And" can also function as a conjunctive. Having it both ways suits the doctrine of the Trinity, where the Spirit is not the Father nor the Son, but is yet the one God. Therefore, not just the generic spirit of God is being confessed, but the subsistent Spirit in substantial relation to the Father. Commentators have also noticed that in the ancient Greek creed of Marcellus of Ancyra there is no definite article before Holy Spirit, leading one to conclude that an earlier meaning referred to the creative spirit of God without necessary reference to the subsistent Holy Spirit.[3] That tension between the spirit of God in history and the Spirit of God in the mystery of the Trinity repeats the debate over the Many and the One that we have pointed to so often as the heart of the mystery of God confessed in the creed, whether in the East or in the West.

The phrase, "Dominum et vivificantem," which follows, lends the Spirit that same status as Jesus who is Lord (*Dominum* in Latin; *Kyrion* in Greek). Just as much as Jesus is Lord, so the Spirit is Lord.

Moreover, the creed confesses that the Spirit gives life; *vivificantem* might be rendered as the "vivifying" or "life-giving" Spirit. This Spirit presides at the births and baptisms unto new life. Where the Spirit blows, there life quickens. Where the Spirit descends, there the desert blooms, the barren become fertile, and the dead come back to life.

The clause, "Who from the Father *and the Son* proceeds" (Qui ex Patre *Filioque* procedit) describes the Trinitarian procession of the Holy Spirit who is God, but God proceeding from the Father who generates the Son, and who together aspirate the Spirit. The theology behind this formulation of the Trinity is largely Augustine's and the West's. The Eastern Church objected to the interpolated phrase, "Filioque," because it declares that the Spirit proceeds both from the Father *and from the Son.* The Greek churchmen objected both from a doctrinal point of view and from the illegitimacy of any interpolation in the ancient creed. Their more acceptable model for the procession of the Holy Spirit was "from the Father and *through the Son.*" Jesus was generated by the Father; the Spirit issues from the Father, but now through the Son. In that sense the Spirit might be understood as "from" the Son. However, the Greek of the classical Niceno-Constantinopolitan Creed makes no mention of a dual procession from the Father and the Son. Moreover, it was argued, John's Gospel says: "When the Advocate comes whom I will send you *from the Father* [emphasis mine], the Spirit of truth that proceeds from the Father, he will testify to me. And you also testify, because you have been with me from the beginning" (15:26). Thus, the interpolation of the "Filioque" was perceived by the Eastern church as an implied criticism of the Nicene Fathers' faith, the ancient and apostolic faith.[4] Indeed, had not the Council of Ephesus (431) forbade further changes in the creed? They held it arrogant to presume to improve upon it.

The "Filioque" probably first appeared at the Council of Toledo (589), and through Gallic France eventually made its way belatedly and even reluctantly into the creed of Rome. The Roman Pontiffs did not at first see the necessity of this addition, and they no doubt saw the divisiveness of such a disputed interpolation. Under pressure of the Roman Emperors, the "Filioque" eventually prevailed even in Rome and despite the long Papal reluctance. Relations between Eastern and Western churches were already long strained. Moreover, the politics of the court of the Holy Roman Empire, which sought ascendancy of the West over the East, was resented. The "Filioque" was the lightning rod that took the force of the gathering storm that finally brought about the great schism of Christendom in 1054. The "Laetentur Caeli" decree of the Council of Florence (1438) tried to affirm one core faith expressed within two legitimate theologies, that of the East and of the West, in the matter of the procession of the Holy Spirit. However, in terms reminiscent of the controversy over "homoousion," the council affirmed the legitimacy of adding "Filioque" to the Western creed. A bold gesture of reconciliation, the Council of Florence nevertheless did not achieve the unity of Christendom, East and West.[5]

The clause "likewise adored and glorified" (simul adoratur et conglorificatur) signifies that the Spirit is worshipped together with and in like manner with the Father and the Son. Just as the Arians made Jesus the greatest of created beings, but less than the one and only God, so there were minimizers of the Holy Spirit. The so-called "Macedonians" or "Pneumatomachi," who were "Arians" of the Spirit, argued that the Holy Spirit was indeed the perfect manifestation of the glory of God in this world. They agreed that the Spirit was of God, holy and from God, but the Spirit was not the one and only God. To the contrary, the creedal language calls for the separation of the "persons" of the Triune God, but declares the equal being of Father, Son, and Spirit, each of whom reveals the face of the one true God in the mystery of the eternal Trinitarian relationships.

The phrase, "Who spoke through the prophets," (qui locutus est per prophetas) validates the manifestation of the same Holy Spirit in the Old Testament. By implication, therefore, all prophets of truth in all times and places participate in the Spirit of God. God is truth. It would have been easy for gentile Christians to reject the Jewish revelation of the Old Testament. The creed affirms that all of sacred history remains the work of the Spirit of the one God "who spoke through the prophets." Similarly, it would be easy for the Christian church to reject the truth of the nations and religions of this world, who also live within the one economy of grace of the one Christ, and who in truth have been given some grasp of the ways of God. The God of the philosophers is not our Lord Jesus Christ, but neither is the truth that philosophy or natural religion can yield about God and God's world in opposition by its very nature with the fullness of truth in the Holy Spirit. "In times past, God spoke in partial and various ways to our ancestors through the prophets; in these last days, he spoke to us through a son, whom he made heir of all things and through whom he created the universe" (Heb. 1:1–2).

The Acts of the Apostles speaks of the Holy Spirit as a fire which gives light and warmth. The spirit illumines our minds and enkindles our hearts. The word "enthusiasm" contains the root word "God" (theos). Consequently we say of the Spirit that it inspires the truth, counsels the doubtful, gives spirited faith and hope to those in darkness. We say of the Spirit that it enlivens our spirit, renews our courage, encourages peace and harmony, gives joy, kindness, generosity, and love of God and neighbor to our cold hearts. Isaiah writes: "And the Spirit of the Lord shall rest upon him, the spirit of wisdom and understanding, the spirit of counsel and might, the spirit of knowledge and the fear of the Lord" (11:2). Such are the charismatic gifts of the Spirit of God. Paul writes: "In contrast, the fruit of the Spirit is love, joy, peace, patience, kindness, generosity, faithfulness, gentleness, self-control" (Gal. 5:22). From the Spirit comes forgiveness of sins, healing of inner wounds, and reconciliation of division. The Spirit of God unifies what has been torn apart, encourages family and community, and fosters the life of the church and the family of humanity under God. The Spirit renews all things and re-creates the face of this earth; the Holy Spirit is the soul of the body of this world. In his wonderful sonnet, "God's Grandeur," Gerard Manley Hopkins concludes:

> And for all this, nature is never spent;
>   There lives the dearest freshness deep down things;
> And though the last lights off the black West went
>   Oh, morning, at the brown brink eastward, springs—
> Because the Holy Ghost over the bent
>   World broods with warm breast and with ah! bright wings.[6]

The scriptures describe the Holy Spirit as the gift of the Father sent by the Son as a comforter or paraclete to abide with the apostles, and to console them on their loss of the earthly Jesus. John writes: "I have told you this while I am with you. The Advocate, the holy Spirit that the Father will send in my name—he will teach you everything and remind you of all that [I] told you" (14:25-26). Even prior to the descent of the Spirit, God has given us the perfect gift, the gift and the giver so intimately compenetrated that the gift embodied the giver. "For God so loved the world that he gave his only Son" (John 3:16). Even human gifts are tokens of the more profound gift which is the giver. Just as the perfect gift embodies the giver, so such a perfect bestowal includes the wherewithal for the reception of the gift. Human lovers court each other; they bide their time and place with care in order that the giving of themselves may entail the welcome reception of the love bestowed. In an eminent way, God gives us both himself and the grace to receive his love. God gives us his only Son and the perfect reception of that self-gift which is the Holy Spirit dwelling in our hearts. Now, giver and gift and reception combine perfectly to accomplish God's life in us—Father and Son and Holy Spirit. Paul concludes his second Letter to the Corinthians: "The grace of the Lord

Jesus Christ and the love of God and the fellowship of the holy Spirit be with all of you" (13:13).

In the Christian doctrine of the Holy Spirit the issue remains whether or not humankind has received the gift of God, or only one of many gifts from God. The gift of the Holy Spirit was cherished not just as a gift of truth and life from God, but as the self-gift of God who is truth and life. Therefore the Spirit has to be God; Jesus has to be Lord. We believe that not only the gifts of God are given to us, but God in God's godness is given to us. We are temples of God, not temples of the manifestations of God and the created gifts of God. We encounter in the third part of the creed the ineffable Spirit of God, that One and infinite mystery of God, who is creator, redeemer, and sanctifier of the Many, and whom we have already apprehended in the earlier parts of the creed.

The Latin liturgy for Pentecost Sunday contained a poetic hymn that functioned as the Sequence. Between the two readings of the scripture, the congregation was invited to meditate on the wonders of the gifts of the Holy Spirit in the world. I will give the poem in the Latin and then render a literal translation; it is impossible to capture in English the beautifully austere turn of phrase that is the genius of the Latin language in this liturgical composition.

Veni Sancte Spiritus et emitte coelitus lucis tuae radium
Veni pater pauperum, veni dator munerum, veni lumen
     cordium
Consolator optime, dulcis hospes animae, dulce refrigerium
In Labore requies, in aestu temperies, in fletu solatium
O lux beatissima, reple cordis intima tuorum fidelium
Sine tuo numine, nihil est in homine, nihil est innoxium
Lava quod est sordidum, riga quod est aridum, sana quod est
     saucium
Flecte quod est rigidum, fove quod est frigidum, rege quod est
     devium
Da tuis fidelibus, in te confidentibus, sacrum septenarium
Da virtutis meritum, da salutis exitum, da perenne gaudium.[7]

Come Holy Spirit and emit the ray of your heavenly light
Come father of paupers, come giver of gifts, come light of hearts
Consoler optimal, sweet guest of the soul, sweet coolness
In work rest, in heat relief, in weeping solace
O light most happy, fill the intimate hearts of your faithful
Without your overshadowing, nothing is in the human, nothing
     is not noxious

Wash what is sordid, water what is arid, heal what is sick
Flex what is rigid, warm what is frigid, rule what is devious
Give to your faithful ones, in you trusting, the sacred seven-fold
Give the merit of virtues, give the outcome of salvation, give peren-
nial joy.

EPILOGUE

Lord of Freedom

The ninth article of the creed declares that the Holy Spirit, who
proceeds from the Father and is sent into the world by the Son to be
our comforter, gently reigns over human freedom, illuminating our
minds and enkindling our hearts. The Spirit is Lord even of the human
heart. The Spirit is sovereign over the reception of God's gift of God's
very self, his very Son. God not only gives the gift; God gives its reception as the first gift, the Spirit who dwells in our hearts. God's
cultivating the mind for the truth and the heart for the good is what
we call grace. No one can outrun the hound of heaven. "Love is strong
as death," says the Song of Songs. What the Holy Spirit wills, the Spirit
will obtain.

What follows for us is this. We do not save ourselves; we do not
even initiate our prayers for help. We are forestalled at every turn by
the Spirit of God who is everywhere. Our good will is already God's
handiwork given to us. But, if God is so for us at every turn, anticipating us and shaping events to fit our needs, who can be against us?
God is like the endlessly resourceful teacher, who can always reach
the recalcitrant student, or like the persevering courting lover, who
will not take "no" for an answer. In the depths of our being, prior to
our consciousness, the Holy Spirit speaks most of all. There God
woos us with infinite resourcefulness to embrace us.

ARTICLE X

To TURN TO THE tenth article: "the holy, catholic church." The immediate insight sees the church as the voluntary gathering of people who come together to worship God. There is fellowship and loyalty to a common endeavor. Many aspects of life, from Sunday school to soup line, come under the roof of this church, sometimes called "holy mother the church."

The further insight sees the church as the convocation of all humankind brought together as a community of brothers and sisters of one Father. The work of the church is thus going on in the hearts of men and women in all places and times. The Holy Spirit inspires love, forgiveness, unity, peace, cooperation, concern for the commonweal, and the welfare of all people of good will. The good will in us is already the work of the Spirit within. Church is thus the constant convocation of the Spirit rather than the work of humankind. The church is temple of the Lord, made up of living stones, and ever being built up into the solidarity of humanity in and with God.

Sanctam Ecclesiam Catholicam

The Latin "sanctam ecclesiam catholicam" means "the holy catholic church." Thus, I believe in the church, which is holy and which is catholic. It does not seem apparent that the church is *holy*, because it is composed of sinners; it does not seem apparent that the church is *catholic* or universal, since the world recognizes no agreed-upon religion and even Christendom suffers divisions. Let us begin with what might be easier to comprehend: the *church* itself as convocation.

The church is a convocation as no other convocation. This assembly is called together by God and convoked from on high. Ultimately the church intends to gather all the nations. This Godly convocation began with the *qahal* of the Hebrew assembly of tribes gathered to form a holy nation, a people set apart by God and for God. In Greek this special community was called the *ekklesia*. The Latin followed the Greek, and from them both we derive in English a word such as "ecclesial." The Germanic word *kirke*, which in turn may be derived from the Greek *kuriake* (belonging to the Lord) gives us in derivation the familiar English word "church."

The oldest versions of the Roman baptismal creed only said "I believe in holy church." In the Latin, the preposition "in" is not found: *credo sanctam ecclesiam*. The Latin, however, supplies this preposition whenever the noun following is God. Thus, *credo in Deum* or *credo in Spiritum Sanctum* (I believe *in* God, or I believe *in* the Holy Spirit). "To believe in" seems to involve an allegiance of the whole being of a person. "To believe in" implies a certain totality and suggests a devotion proper only toward God. Rufinus of Aquileia wished to make this point in his early commentary on the creed.[1] Accordingly, the creed confesses its acknowledgment of the church and its belief, but does not make the church a loyalty to be compared with what belongs to God. The church is always provisional, and in the New Jerusalem we will no longer need church services. God is in the church, but the church is not God.

The church remains primarily a convocation called by God. "City of God," not of this world, the church yet remains in this world and the "city of man." The church visible accumulates a history that brings about the Kingdom of God, but it never in this life becomes equivalent to the Kingdom of God. Nonetheless, the church does point to

118

the Kingdom of God and its inception here and now. The church on earth should be seen as means to that end. The church in this life must also suffer and die along with its Lord and King who died on the cross. Then the church will rise with Christ to enter the Kingdom of God. Only this church of the end time, however, will represent amply and adequately the Kingdom of God.

While it remains true that to be Christian is not simply equivalent to being in the church, we cannot become fully Christian without the Christian community which is the church. Helmut Thielicke turns a helpful sentence when he writes: "We are not Christians so that there can be a church; there is a church so that we can be Christians, thereby gaining our salvation."[2] To be a loving person is more important than to be a member of a church, although to become loving depends upon belonging to other people in responsibility to them and for them. Our ecclesiology declares that we are saved in and through the community, and our anthropology understands that the group can contribute enormously to the development of the individual. The Hebrew nomads in the desert knew well that survival in a hostile land was impossible without the support of the whole tribe. The church represents an ark of salvation in a sea of woes. The church is family wherein the members are carried one by the other, and each depends on the other in season and out. No matter how much one's behavior is a burden, each of us remains always "family." Fellowship in the church points to a profound idea of communal salvation. We literally save one another.

Nonetheless, all community, as all family, must be constantly reformed (semper reformanda) that it may truly continue to serve the individual welfare of the group member, who must not only serve the group but also be served by the group. Only the grace of God can fully resolve this perennial tension and do justice both to the pursuits of the individual for his or her own fulfillment, and the service of and devotion to the church as "mother of the living" that crowns Christian life as self-giving love.

The creed affirms belief in the church as the assembly of people convoked by the Holy Spirit, who invites them, unites them, and enlivens them as a community in and of the spirit of God. Thus the Holy Spirit is the soul-life of the body of human beings which is the church. The Spirit is the bond that makes the members of the church into the mystical body of Jesus Christ who is Lord, and thereby members of one another. In the church, the Holy Spirit dwells as in a temple. Therefore, this house, made up of living stones, made up of the people whom God has graced, should be known as a *holy* temple. Filled with the *holy* spirit, the assembly that is the church deserves to be called a *holy* temple.

One must first believe in the Holy Spirit, of course, before one could be expected to believe in the assembly of the Spirit. One must believe in the Holy Spirit, "Lord and life-giver," before one could be expected to believe in the holiness of the people convoked by that same Spirit. God's love is not attracted primarily by the goodness of creatures. Rather it is their need to exist and the poverty of their resources for life and goodness that call out to the Father Almighty. God does not move toward the goodness in another as human desire draws close to the other for its fulfillment. God's love is creative of goodness. Whom God loves becomes good. God's mercy seeks how to bring good in abject need. God's world is indeed a welfare state. After each day of creation in the Genesis story, God pronounced that "it was good." The Holy Spirit that sanctifies the assembly that is the church creates a goodness and holiness that depend on the church being recipient of God's initiative.

In such a church, the good ethics of the membership will not establish a "holy" church, for the church must always be from above. Only the holiness of God indwelling in the church of sinners will bring about the holiness of its members. Grace is ever from above, and it is promised without fail (ex opere operato).[3] God's irrevocable love will be given unto us, not as a reward for good behavior, but as God's merciful response to the need and misery of all human behavior. The church always remains a gift received; the fulfillment of the Law is not its boast. Just as from the fullness of the Creator we have received, so from the fullness of the holiness of the Spirit we receive. Ethics is a seeking God from below; worship and thanksgiving are drawn forth by God from above. Thus, the *holy* church remains always God's work. The Spirit assembles from a no-church a people, who are holy in the first instance precisely because they are "set apart" and called to be God's own people. In the First Letter of Peter we read: "But you are 'a chosen race, a royal priesthood, a holy nation, a people of his own, so that you may announce the praises' of him who called you out of darkness into his wonderful light. Once you were 'no people' but now you are God's people; you 'had not received mercy' but now you have received mercy" (2:9–10). This doctrine does not deny that the Spirit also sanctifies the church by the works of virtue in its members. Church liturgy nourishes the life of holiness in its participants, and it is never a substitute for everyday virtues. The church has never been indifferent to the witness of the saints who proclaim

God not only intends holiness but achieves it in his loved ones in ways varied and marvelous to behold.

The word "holiness" has been readily associated with "wholeness." The fullness of human virtue and development ought to be fostered by the church rightly understood, for it seeks through the gift of the holiness of God to achieve the holiness and wholeness of all humanity as God intends it to be. In Jesus we have seen what human nature might become, when attuned to the ways of God. Our model of humanity remains this Jesus, and not Apollo. The imitation of Christ Jesus beckons all Christians to pursue their own sanctity and thus their humanity. "For when two or three are gathered together in my name, there am I in the midst of them" (Mt. 18:20).

The inclusion of the adjective "catholic" together with "holy" represents a somewhat later addition to the established text. The holy, *catholic* (katholika in Greek) church portrays the universal or general church of humankind before the one God who always regards it. The solidarity of the human race flows from its God-given bodily existence; humanity is ever and obviously interdependent. The family is a microcosm of the macrocosm that is the church. God determined to give life to humankind as a people, called together now not so much by blood as by the water of faith that makes spiritual kin. Jesus is one of us, and therefore Lord, bringing into his kingdom everyone of us. His salvation belongs to all the people of the earth. Hence the catholic church ought to be an over-arching and all-embracing umbrella community that spans the centuries and the continents. The catholic church lays claim to be the "great church," that embraces all local churches in a world community bond. The community known as the catholic church is the catholic church insofar as it gathers together all of the living and the dead under the one Lord and King. At its best the church yearns to embrace everyone; it desires to exclude no one.

The very word "catholic" means universal. It connotes non-elitist, non-exclusive, non-provincial. Catholic means cosmopolitan, striving to be all things to all men and women. One of the Old English creeds translates the Latin with the English "holy *general* church."[4] The catholic church is the genus, and the local churches the species. Just as a contemporary full-opportunity employer, the church declares itself open without discrimination due to age, race, color, sex, and insofar as possible even creed. Jesus mingled with sinners and outcasts. The unity of the church will sometimes be burdened with bearing each other's burdens. About such ecumenicity there will be controversy. Yet surely the church must be tolerant, non-judgmental, welcoming, while ever guarding the integrity of its own apostolic witness and the legitimate claims of the truth as it has been given to know it. Openness to all while yet claiming one's own identity has ever been a difficult balance to achieve. An eclectic syncretism is not catholic, nor is a ghetto-like chauvinism. Beyond nations, beyond sects, beyond ideologies, catholic is never beyond truth.

The church at its best collects people, just as the Collect of the Eucharistic liturgy collects the silent prayers of the assembled faithful. The church ought to be a sign lifted up among the nations, a light placed on a lampstand. It is sinful, yet holy without blemish. It remains in this world, yet "I have conquered the world" (John 16:33). The Kingdom of God is now, for the Holy Spirit dwells in our hearts and eternal life is given us today in faith. And yet, the Kingdom of God is then, in the eschaton, when the Holy Spirit will have filled the temple and captured the hearts of all the faithful, who will then see God as God is, face to face.

That the church takes for its scope all that is human follows from this catholicity of the church. A Christian humanism can incorporate all of creation, because all human culture in its goodness, and all human beings in their destiny, are touched by the unfailing grace of the Holy Spirit that ever gives life to the world-church. Christians believe in such a catholic humanism, because they believe in the humanity of Jesus Christ. The church hopes to encompass the whole of human history and all the nations, because it ultimately believes the Son of God was truly enfleshed, one man fully human like us. All creation and all human endeavors draw close to the Word of God incarnate, because nothing truly human is evermore alien to God who was so embodied in our days, and "for our sake and for our salvation."

The first generation of Christians faced the problem of universality in the church in terms of the inclusion of the Gentiles. To become a follower of Jesus Christ, must one become a Jew? That became the issue of catholicity. Peter and Paul are described in Acts in debate over the universal mission of the Christian church. Were all the nations included in God's plan of salvation, and under what terms of conversion? The outcome moved finally in favor of the Gentiles without prejudice to the Jewish Christians. In our contemporary world, Christians face the problem of universality in the church in terms of the inclusion of the non-Western world. To become Christian must one become Western? Karl Rahner thought it was the central issue for Catholicism.[5] Some think the issue involves the full incorporation of women in the church. It would seem that the matter of universality manifests once again the theme of the mystery of the One and the Many. Jesus who is Lord encompasses in one infinite Being the quasi-infinite variety of this many-splendored creation. The one church that is the one body of the Lord tries to comprehend in its embrace this bountiful many. The holiness of the many depends upon the one Holy Spirit, just as the existence of the many depends upon the one Almighty Father.

The Nicene Creed adds two notes to the creed: "*one*, holy catholic, and *apostolic* church." These four adjectives have traditionally defined the nature of the church. The four words overlap in meaning, somewhat like the four verbs: "suffered, was crucified, was dead, and was buried." As we shall see below, the Nicene Creed does not include the "communion of saints," which phrase may contain some of the understanding of oneness and mission for the spiritual welfare of others that these two added "notes" suggest in the Eastern Creed. Both words appeal to the unity of the church over against a divided Christianity. Both appeal to integrity and consistency of teaching and religious practice. Indeed, the profession of faith in an *apostolic* church, whose origins are traced to the apostles and which hopes to preserve such a heritage, reflects the controversy surrounding the composition of the Conciliar Creed.

The Council of Nicaea was convened by the Emperor Constantine precisely to guarantee the unity of the church as an important component of the needed unity of the Roman Empire. That unification of local churches was to be cultivated by the common unity, or community, of the local bishops assembled in general or ecumenical council. Episcopal collegiality and concord would preserve the legitimate pluralism in the churches that were planted in diverse cultures, and yet foster the desired unity of the "great church," now recognized officially by the great empire. Nonetheless, this longed-for unity does not come about solely by the insertion of the right words into the profession of faith. Rather, the unity of the church as always stems from the unique bond with the one sovereign Lord, whose only beloved Son became human, that all people of all ages, past and future, might be effectively invited into the one Kingdom of God. Such is finally the work of the Holy Spirit that animates the church while also breathing wheresoever it wills. Although many people and many religions make up the world, there remains one only God and one name through which we are all saved. Jesus reigns as Lord of all, whether or not that name is uttered by the lips of faith or embraced incognito by a heart of faith in God. Jesus prayed for the unity of the church: "And I have given them the glory you gave me, so that they may be one, as we are one, I in them and you in me, that they may be brought to perfection as one, that the world may know that you sent me, and that you loved them even as you loved me" (John 17: 22–23).

The disunity of the Christendom, therefore, must be seen as a scandal in which all the divided churches bear a share of the responsibility. We have all sinned. And yet, perhaps as never before, Christian churches need each other and have been driven by the traumatic historical events of this century to seek the deeper bond of unity that has always been present in the general acceptance of Jesus as Lord. The widespread cooperation and ecumenical tone in biblical studies may prove a harbinger.

Non-Christian religions and unchurched populations far outnumber those who belong to the visible church. "No salvation outside of the church" cannot mean that these people, who are the vast majority of the human race, are excluded from God's salvation, intended for all and unavailable to them in most cases through no fault of their own. Either we must conclude that the Holy Spirit attracts hearts to God independently of the church, which never exhausts the resourcefulness and boundlessness of the ways of the infinite and mysterious God, or we must conclude that many people who know not of the church are yet somehow included in its membership and embraced in some hidden way. Their membership in the church awaits its full, visible bodily expression. Baptism of desire yearns for its expression in the community of baptism of water. Nevertheless, all are baptized in the one Spirit unto life eternal with the one true God. In short, Jesus died for all people once and for all, and the Holy Spirit is given for everyone.

Undergirding the hope of *one* church is the claim of one foundation. The church stems from the apostles, who were witnesses in the beginning of Jesus Christ who was from above. Thus, the "one, holy, catholic" church must also be the *apostolic* church. All Christian churches, of course, wish to be founded only upon the faith of the apostles. No Christian church (the Mormons excepted) claims to trace its origin to anyone beside the early community that knew the Lord and were chosen to be with him. The "deposit of faith" remains a sacred trust and treasure of the church, guarded by divine safe-keeping, so that even "the gates of the netherworld shall not prevail against it" (Mt. 16:18). The dispute over the primacy of Peter is not an argument over apostolic foundation, but rather over the hierarchical arrangement of that one foundation. The search for a graceful implementation of the primacy of Peter presents the churches with a mirror that reflects the imperfections connected with all human arrangements. Greater than our divisions, however, is the unity of the grace of God, and in that hope may the churches continue to seek to be fully apostolic according to the scriptures.

"Apostolic" does not suggest only a mission backward to that origin that guarantees the integrity of the Gospel entrusted to the early church. The word also proclaims that the apostolic church is sent forward on a mission to share the good news of Jesus Christ with all the world. Just as the apostles were commissioned to preach to the whole world, so is the church called to be apostolic in its service of humanity. Jesus came "not to be served but to serve." Social justice may be an end in itself, but for the church such liberation must also be a means to proclaim the good news that unites all people as the children of one God. Clearly Vatican II affirms the church has a mission to the modern world.[6] The church never disowns its own apostolicity more than when it is caught up in its own concerns that amount to a form of self-serving. When the church wishes to protect only its privileges, and not to extend hand and heart to those outside its present bounds, then the church lays little claim to be *apostolic*. "Go, therefore, and make disciples of all nations, baptizing them in the name of the Father, and of the Son, and of the holy Spirit, teaching them to observe all that I have commanded you. And behold, I am with you always, until the end of the age" (Mt. 28:19–20).

In the church's service of the world and in its mission to save the world, in the primarily spiritual manner that a church can claim, the community of Jesus Christ does not pretend to bring about the Kingdom now and Heaven here below. What the church does will never equal or exhaust all that God does. Nevertheless, while the church awaits the fullness of the Kingdom there and then, it labors mightily to save human beings from all that is evil, wrong, and destructive, here and now. Albert Van Den Heuvel writes:

> The Scripture only says that the church is many things—people, bride, salt, light. The New Testament employs ninety-six different symbols! This discovery marked the beginning of a theology of renewal: *the church is manifold*. Church means many things at the same time, and this is bound up with the fact that the Church cannot be relegated to a corner of our private lives. The church is a new kind of life. Then there was a second discovery: The church is not a place or primarily an institution; *she is an event*, an activity. We do not belong to the church; we are the church. The church is not organized; she is called, she is a way,

she happens. This idea is bound up with the fact that God has called the church not for her own sake, but for the sake of the world. And so the third discovery was that the *church is mission*. Mission is not simply one of her many activities, for the church herself is a function of God's mission in the world; she has been called to announce God's good news of hope, of the open future, of the victory over humanity. She is to announce this message, retell it, exemplify it, and keep it alive, just as Jesus did.[7]

The tenth article of the creed says something not only about the church, but also about God and about human beings. With reference to God, "one, holy, catholic, and apostolic," declares: (1) the one only God who creates and redeems the world, (2) the Spirit that sanctifies the church in the world, (3) Jesus Christ Our Lord who took all that is human unto himself, and (4) the one world loved in its entirety by God and to whom the church is sent to minister salvation. With reference to humankind, "one, holy, catholic, and apostolic" declares: (1) the unity of creation, (2) the indwelling of the Holy Spirit in the hearts of men and women, (3) the acceptance of all being as worthy of being saved and brought into the Kingdom, and (4) the commission to serve the needs of humankind that is constitutive of the church and given in baptism to all Christians.

The "catholicity" of the church implies its *oneness*, for to be catholic is to be world-wide in embrace, all-inclusive in space and time even to the ends of the earth. The "holiness" of the church implies its *apostolic* origin, for to be holy is to be in contact with the source of all holiness who is Jesus the Lord, and to be pointed toward the end of the mission when time yields to the triumph of the Holy Spirit that draws the church home to the thrice-holy God. In Paul's Letter to the Ephesians we read:

> For this reason I kneel before the Father, from whom every family in heaven and on earth is named, that he may grant you in accord with the riches of his glory to be strengthened with power through his Spirit in the inner self, and that Christ may dwell in your hearts through faith; that you, rooted and grounded in love, may have strength to comprehend with all the holy ones what is the breadth and length and height and depth, and to know the love of Christ that surpasses knowledge, so that you may be filled with all the fullness of God. Now to him who is able to accomplish far more than all we ask or imagine, by the power

at work within us, to him be glory in the church and in Christ Jesus to all generations, forever and ever. Amen. (3:14–21)

EPILOGUE

Lord of Community

The tenth article of the creed declares that the Holy Spirit is Lord of the community of humankind. Jesus knew a particular solidarity with the human race. Human beings, whether or not they know it, remain ever in a state of interdependence. Hell is to be alone with only me; heaven is to be altogether with always we. God is Lord of community. The trinitarian life of God is interpersonal sharing. The Holy Spirit is Lord of church. Because the Spirit is Lord of our freedom, the Spirit is also Lord of our cooperation, our gathering into family, our solidarity and bondedness as partakers of the same human nature, our common destiny, our human condition as inter-sharing beings. We do not so much compete with each other for genuine life as we enhance and contribute to the further happiness of one another. Truth and love are not diminished by being shared; they are multiplied for everyone. This community life we celebrate in church. The Spirit convokes that collaboration and common union; the Spirit is the Lord of community, of the One that gathers finally the Many.

For us what follows is this. I can only be me, when we are we. Conversely, we can only be us, when me is me. The individual and the group need not be opposed in church. Full justice ought to be done to both. The individual gives to the group; the community serves the unique person before God that each of us always remains. The church is thus both particular and general, just as its judgment remains both particular (individual) and general (communal) in the fulfillment of the age to come.

ARTICLE XI

TO TURN TO THE eleventh article: "the communion of saints, the forgiveness of sins." The immediate insight sees the assembled saints in the church surrounding us with their love and intercession as grandparents do. Into that ancient fellowship we have been invited. Because our sins have been forgiven in the sacraments, we grow in the holiness of the saints. The Church Militant on earth strives for the sinlessness of the Church Triumphant in heaven. Together with the Church Suffering (in Purgatory) all the saints press on toward the fullness of the Kingdom of God.

The further insight sees the greatest miracle of God in the conversion of the human heart from the self-centered isolation that is sin to the common-good-centered communion that is the church forgiven. Forgiveness is the creation of "we," where no "we" existed before. To bring good out of evil is to create from opposition. The communion of saints and the forgiveness of sins is a creation from less than nothing. So sovereign is the goodness of God, that the Spirit creates good even from evil and the hard-heartedness of sin. God writes straight with crooked lines. Everything serves God's purposes for good, even sins.

Communionem Sanctorum

The Latin "communionem sanctorum" means "the communion of saints." Within the holy church there is a saintly common union. Within the holy church there is a fellowship of the membership. That common bond is based upon the holiness of the people of God and the holiness of the things of God which they share together. It is tempting to want to explain the "communion of saints" by appealing to something simpler and more fundamental. Accordingly, one might speak of the union of members of one family who live with each other and for each other, one for all and all for one. Or, appeal might be made to the bond of union between lovers, which allows them to see their own welfare as inevitably joined to their partner's. However helpful such comparisons may be, it would seem that the "communion" experienced in the church goes beyond all of them. While it includes emotional ties, this communion transcends them. It does not preclude material support, but neither does it require such goods. Large group togetherness reveals something of the "communion of saints," but does not exhaust its richness. Soldiers have known a special fellowship under fire, and monks and nuns experience community life among many companions. The vowed life in the church gives witness to the appeal of a fully shared life with commitment from the group and to it. The "communion of saints," however, remains unique and incomparable.

Some commentators suggest that the Greek expression of "communion," which is *koinonia*, offers an irreducible paradigm of this mystery. The English word, "fellowship," the Russian word *sobornost*, the Latin *convivium* come to mind as rough equivalents. However, Paul's theology of the church as the body of Christ presents an even richer understanding. Extended through time and space, the Christian community continues the life and ministry of Jesus; Christians make up the mystical body of Christ. By his life they live, and together they share with each other all they have received from their Lord. What is one's own has been received from Christ, and thus it should be shared in Christ. "What do you possess that you have not received? But if you have received it, why are you boasting as if you did not receive it?" (1 Cor. 4:7). Consequently, we share with each other the Christ we have received. We share together in Christ. Jesus Christ is the bond that links the community which makes up his body, mem-

130

bers one of the other. Thus we need each other. We help each other, just as members of a living body are organically interdependent. To the Corinthians Paul says: "If [one] part suffers, all the parts suffer with it; if one part is honored, all the parts share its joy. Now you are Christ's body, and individually parts of it" (1 Cor. 12:26–27). The communion of saints is none other than the body of Christ, and the body of Christ is now the church, the assembly of the people of God.

One cannot believe in the communion of saints as shared life — the bonding of close community, the membership in a living body, the synergetic solidarity—unless one has previously believed in the "holy church." And one cannot believe that a group of disparate people can become an organic body with exchanged inner life, unless one has previously believed in the Holy Spirit. The very soul of the body and the convoking spirit of the assembly is its source of life and unity. Thus the articles of the creed build upon each other. The later ones presuppose the earlier ones. The Spirit founds the church, and the church supports the communion of saints.

The phrase, "communion of saints," is not found in the eastern creeds. Nor is it found in the western creeds until after the fourth century. Some commentators attribute its introduction to Nicetas of Remesiana.[1] However that may be, the phrase remains a late-established addition to the creed, but one nonetheless rich with meaning for the formulation of Christian faith. Furthermore, western creeds are divided whether to construe the phrase "the holy catholic church, [which is] the communion of saints," or to start the next article with "the communion of saints and the forgiveness of sins." The discussion below will explain this controversy.

The Latin "communionem sanctorum," would allow for two readings: (1) the common union of *holy people* who are the saints (masculine gender reading of "sanctorum"), or (2) the common union in *holy things*, which are primarily the sacraments (neuter gender reading of "sanctorum"). Following the first reading, the faithful are bonded in solidarity as saints filled with the one Spirit; following the second, they share in holy things, particularly the sacraments and especially the Eucharist. Holy Communion unites the church around one table, one bread, one faith, one body, and one Lord. Both meanings are valid, although the English translation would seem to favor holy people over holy things. One of the translations of the creed in Old French renders the Latin as *communion des seintes choses*, which would favor holy things.[2]

If we read the "communion of *saints*" as *sancti* or holy people, what might we conclude? The church is a living body, the body of

Christ, whose soul is the Holy Spirit. Church solidarity spans time and space, and even transcends them. Accordingly, Christians are united with each other and share a common life. The good reverberates in all of us; the evil is suffered by everyone. This communion perdures despite our bodies being in different places and times. The Church Militant struggling on this earth nonetheless communes with the church not on this earth. Time is not cut off from eternity. Those who have died and gone before us are alive in the body of the church, whether they belong to the Church Triumphant in heaven that looks on the face of God, or the Church Suffering which awaits purification to enter into the fullness of salvation. The dead who died in grace belong to the church of God, who is God of the dead as well as the living, and whose will is done in heaven and on earth. The altars of the early Christians were built upon the tombs of the martyrs, and so the faithful thought to call upon the intercession of these saints in heaven. They believed that through the communion of saints they could gain the grace of God from the martyrs of yesterday. Perhaps the communion of saints could not be properly and fully understood from the beginning, because the impact of Christian martyrdom in the church was yet to be experienced widely.

Only people live forever. The Christian church does not consist of stones that, however hard, will turn to dust from the erosion of time. Our church is built of living stones that, however vulnerable in their flesh, will never perish. The stained glass windows crowded with the cathedral saints remind us in vivid color that the saints in heaven join us in the same praise of almighty God. They are like grandparents, who stand by faithfully day and night, in better or in worse, faithful and caring to us no matter what the circumstances of our life. United with them, Christians say with all the angels of heaven gathered around the throne of God: "Holy, holy, holy is the Lord of hosts" (Is. 6:3). The dead who live in God join us in the Eucharist that will never end. They await us. They belong to us, and their prayers assist us. Through the intercession of the saints we are drawn closer into their communion with God. Our ancestors and our beloved dead are alive in the one holy church. Jan Milic Lochman writes: "Ecumenicity is historical as well as geographical."[3] At solemn moments, such as the baptisms celebrated at the Easter Vigil, the community intones the "Litany of the Saints." With them all we have communion in the church. The past is not obliterated; it is only hidden in God.

On earth we pray also for the "souls" of the departed, who await the purgation of the remnants of their sins. While it is difficult to imagine a purgatory without our categories of extension of place and duration of time, yet we can affirm that the prayers of the living rise up, and not in vain, for the dying and for the dead. If the prayers of the saints in heaven can benefit the "saints" on earth, why cannot the prayers of the living reach out to the dead? Intercessory prayer is a confession of a faith that believes the infinite and sovereign God comprehends all of the past, present, and future. In the One, the Many are never far apart. We are all members of one body, whose head is Christ. We dwell all together in the Holy Spirit, whose temple we are. How appropriate a paraphrase of the "communion of saints" were we to call upon the "solidarity of the saints." St. Paul writes: "As a body is one though it has many parts, and all the parts of the body, though many, are one body, so also Christ. For in one Spirit we were all baptized into one body, whether Jews or Greeks, slaves or free persons, and we were all given to drink of one Spirit" (1 Cor. 12:12–13).

If we read the "communion of saints" as *sancta* or holy things, what might we conclude? Communion in the church takes place through the commonly shared sacraments. In baptism Christians are born into the living body of the church. They must be fed at the common Eucharistic table of the Lord, if they are to grow in this new life. Since a Christian can be born only once, the Nicene Creed confesses "one baptism for the forgiveness of sins." Although liturgical ceremony may bring to mind baptism with water, and even infant baptism for most Christians, the essence of baptism remains the indwelling of the Holy Spirit. Baptism with water is the visible and communal sign of that inner change of heart. Thus, the third part of the creed affirms belief in the Spirit who brings to birth the life of Christ in the catechumen; the "communion of saints" begins to speak of the impact of that new birth. Communion with holy people in the church and with holy things in the sacraments that reconcile reveals how the self-isolation and self-denigration of our sins has truly been forgiven. The very "we-ness" of the church community is the demonstration of the overcoming and forgiving of sin, which divides the human race.

The Byzantine liturgy begins its distribution of Holy Communion with this line: "Holy things for holy people." The church itself is the great sacrament, in which we all together commune. In the Eucharist the common life of the mystical body of Christ is fed and nourished by the sacramental body of the Lord. We live by his life. Jesus is the greatest sacrament. He is "the way, the truth, and the life." We call this eating of the Eucharistic bread a Holy Communion. Baptism is but the gateway to all of the other sacraments, and the sacraments all culminate in the Eucharist. Here is the perfect sacrament, the efficacious sign that reveals the church as convocation of the

Spirit. Thus it is most clearly and most intensely church around the table of the body of the Lord.

Friendship with each other, as wonderful as that may be, does not constitute the church. We do not think that our deeds of mutual goodness one for the other are the true cause of our salvation. We believe that it is fellowship in Christ that makes for fellowship with each other, and that it remains the *gesta Dei* (the deeds of God) that give efficacy to our own deeds of virtue. In the Eucharist, the communion of saints and the communion of sacraments becomes the holy communion of the people of God gathered around a common table of the Lord in anticipation and in foretaste of the eternal banquet in the kingdom that is to come. Then shall we all be one, "I in them and you in me, that they may be brought to perfection as one, that the world may know that you sent me, and that you loved them even as you loved me" (John 17:23).

Those who believe that the "communion of saints" is shorthand for the church of holy people argue that the phrase amplifies and paraphrases what it means to believe in the church of the Spirit. In other words, belief in the Holy Spirit and the gift (or baptism) of the Spirit leads to membership in the holy community (the church). That condition can be described as the communion of saints. Those who believe that the phrase in question refers to the sacraments argue that the "communion of saints" is an introduction to the sacramental life of the church. It points to the "forgiveness of sins," which is the effect of all the sacraments. In other words, the sacramental life of the church brings about the forgiveness of sins and the reconciliation of all peoples. The issue does not touch primarily the forgiveness of sins that the individual may be consciously guilty of, although that restoration surely is included. Rather the "communion of saints" reveals the reconciliation of those perennial divisions and antagonisms among human beings that are the result of sin and its manifestation. Thus the "communion of saints" leads to the overcoming of all alienation and can be described as the "forgiveness of sins."

Study of the divisions of the creed might lead one to conclude that the Protestant tradition is more comfortable with the "communion of saints" as the people of the church, whereas the Catholic tradition favors the sacraments of the church. Exception to that convenient polarization can readily be found, however. Since the effect of baptism is the outpouring of the Spirit and the forgiveness of sins, it may be possible to combine both interpretations into one. Looking backward the communion of saints views the Holy Spirit as the bond of unity, and looking forward it sees the forgiveness of sins as the result of that unity. The outpouring of the Spirit thus creates communion, which in turn creates forgiveness and reconciliation. As we will see below, that forgiveness leads in turn to the resurrection of the body and life everlasting. When self-entanglement is overcome in forgiveness, and the community is established in harmony around its source that is the Lord of life, then the body cannot die and the relationships among the children of God cannot lead to dead ends. Thus the third part of the creed catalogs the effects of grace, the ever-opening doors into God, all the result of the descent of the Holy Spirit upon the apostles. Jesus who is the great sacrament of God leaves to us the church which is his body and the great sacrament we can encounter, and the church as the great sacrament reconciles both meanings of this pivotal creedal phrase.

Remissionem Peccatorum

The Latin "remissionem peccatorum" means "the forgiveness of sins." The Christian believes in forgiveness, indeed in the very possibility of forgiveness. The Christian believes that human beings remain "tangled lovers," however distorted and sinful their present behavior. God created humankind good, and sin is a distortion. The Christian believes that only God can judge, fairly and completely, the visible and the invisible, and that God does so with both justice and mercy. Nonetheless, there is no justice in this world. Innocent children suffer outrage; guilty men and women receive gifts of love and grace they could never deserve even if sinless. Human beings always receive less than they deserve, and at the same time more than they deserve. The unearned and gratuitous love of God that is showered upon us outweighs the mysterious and presently unexplained sufferings of this life that are rarely proportioned to a person's deeds. What forgiveness claims is that love is more ultimate than justice, and that a forgiving heart is more important than evening the score.

The Christian also believes that God's forgiveness knows no limits. Seventy times seven we are to forgive, as urged by Jesus in the Gospels. If God now punishes, God then saves. To err may be human; to forgive is divine. If anyone insists, alas, upon a final and unrelenting, unforgiving condition, it must be nothing of God's. There is not a vindictive moment in our God, nor should there be in the hearts of his people. That forgiveness is truly possible, especially for people who have suffered mighty injury, remains an act of faith that flows from the previous affirmations of this creed. The followers of the tortured and crucified Jesus proclaim that he said when dying: "Father, forgive them, they know not what they do" (Luke 23:34).

In the Gospels, Jesus mingles with the sinners of his society. He says he came "to call sinners." It is the sick who need the physician, and not the well. He speaks of the tax collectors and the prostitutes entering the Kingdom of God first, because they know their sinfulness. To them was given the Kingdom, because they were in such need. Yet, all men and women have sinned. No one casts the first stone in the story of the woman taken in adultery (see John 8). We all fall short of the glory of our humanity. We miss the mark; we go astray; we fail to bring to completion the humanity we have begun.

The Greek word for sin is *hamartia*, which literally means to miss the mark, just as an arrow fails to hit its target. Our sin can be called our failure to reach out and to respect and love all of God's creation. Our sin reflects the walls we have constructed to overcome our fear that this vulnerable flesh will suffer pain long before it dies, and will perish utterly. Our sin proclaims that *we* are all we have; there is no God who loves and protects us. Our sin is the pathetic drawing around us the wagons of our life in a fearful self-encirclement that represents our peculiar egocentricity. We are thus "tangled lovers," who mean well but who do not know where the true enemy is nor where the true friend. In attempting to secure our own best interests, we destroy them. Nonetheless, our sinfulness never reflects our true intentions nor gives expression to our best selves. We miss our mark; our intention is an arrow gone wide. We had not meant to lose our life or condemn others to lose theirs. Perhaps there does exist a malice that goes beyond this error of sin, even if error is understood to be in the heart and will just as much as in the head. If so, such malice is incomprehensible. The sins that we can understand, although we must not excuse them, do readily call forth forgiveness. Hence we believe in the communion of saints by the power of the Holy Spirit, and the "forgiveness of sins."

God loved us first, says St. Paul, and while we were yet sinners. Jesus gathered the disciples into his fellow travelers and intimate company despite their sinfulness. He remained in communion with them despite their ultimate flight and betrayal of him. It is not forgiveness of sins that precedes fellowship, as if I deign to forgive my brother or sister in a patronizing way, so that they may be worthy of my friendship and acceptable in my circle of acquaintance. Rather, forgiveness is a love that goes out to unattractive sinners, to include them and to embrace them in the communion of saints (read sinners) that leads to reconciliation, the forgiveness of sins, and the conversion of the unrepentant. We are not forgiven primarily because we repent. Rather, because we in turn forgive our brother and sister, it becomes evident that our hearts have been softened and we have thus repented. "Forgive us our trespasses as we forgive those who trespass against us" does not declare the initiative is ours. The "Our Father" does not declare "forgive us *because* we forgive others," but rather that insofar as we forgive others we proclaim how much we have accepted our own forgiveness.

Surely we are a sinful people. What we need to know is that we are unconditionally accepted. That would be good news and that would be the heart of good news. Most of us believe if we were really known, we would not be loved. That is not the good news of the Gospels. At the same time, behavior does indeed make a difference, and we all know this. God's solution to our need to be accepted as we are and yet to be made good is unique. God's love does not wait for goodness to appear in the beloved in order to be thus attracted. Rather, God is drawn close by our need, poverty, and misery. God's goodness urges God, and such a love goes out to us while we are yet sinners. God's love makes goodness appear in us. Forgiveness is another face of genuine love. God's love is always creative of good. Even the pagans love their friends who do good to them in return; Christians were challenged by Jesus Christ to love their enemies, to do good to those who persecuted them. Then there would be no ambiguity about their motivation. Then the splendor of the love of God that shines on the good and on the bad, and which has been poured out in the hearts of those who know the Spirit, would be apparent in this world. When love touches a person's heart, and that gift is not predicated on behavior that must earn it, such love evokes a change of heart. It is a forgiving love that allows sinners to accept being who they are. Now they are neither being tolerated or condemned, but deeply loved and invited to respond. Their conversion would seem to be a response of gratitude to an offer made to them without self-serving calculation.

At the end of the creed we may seem to be a long way from the creation story in the beginning. And yet, the "forgiveness of sins" is the new and almighty creation story. God the Father creates life now, not out of nothing, but even out of evil and out of sinfulness. The conversion of the human heart and its freedom is a greater creation than a physical universe. Creation out of sinfulness is more marvelous than creation from nothingness. To love one's enemies is more marvelous than to move the stars. The creed draws to a close with the affirmation that human beings need not remain only self-serving, paralyzed by fear and clinging to whatever part of the creation seems to offer salvation. They need not be rapacious and driven to cling to their own interests because they believe they are godless and thus they are on their own. The creed prepares us to receive forgiveness, to break down our barriers and alienation, to move into reconciliation. Thus we become church, the communion of saints that leads to the forgiveness of sins. Now there is a "we" to replace the lonesome "I," and now there is a common world, God's world, filled with God, and proclaiming that we live, not on our own, but together in God's own life.

The Nicene Creed adds "*one baptism* for the forgiveness of sins." The Acts of the Apostles gives us these words of Peter: "Repent and be baptized every one of you, in the name of Jesus Christ for the forgiveness of your sins; and you will receive the gift of the holy Spirit" (2:38). In the forgiveness of sins, neither creed addresses the recurrent and on-going need for forgiveness that is acknowledged in the beginning of every Eucharistic celebration as well as in the ordinary sacrament of Penance. Forgiveness along the way of our daily life is more remedial; it is hospital care, and even critical care at times. Such forgiveness, however, is not the baptismal creation of new life. Rather, it is the restoration of life that was once and for all given in Jesus Christ and publicly acknowledged in baptism. Both creeds talk of this more fundamental reconciliation, which is the sacrament of baptism, one time and forever, the indelible seal upon the Christian who is incorporated in the Spirit-filled risen body of Christ that is the church.

In that church we are brother and sister to each other and our kinship in the one Spirit of God can never be erased. Paul writes of one body, one faith, one bread, one Lord of all. The incarnation of Jesus reveals the love of God made available to all humankind. The definitive forgiveness of the world's sins, which culminates on the cross in a love unsurpassable, leads to communion with the crucified Lord unto the resurrection of the body. Jesus is the great sacrament, the one sacrament; the church is the on-going Jesus in time and space; the sacrament of baptism is the on-going church; the sacrament of penance the on-going baptism. Whether or not people come to the Church visible, whether or not they call on Jesus by his proper name, whether or not they achieve baptism of water, if they are to be forgiven unto eternal life, they belong to the church that is the body of Jesus. In their hearts they love Jesus the Christ, whom they never knew. They are baptized in their desire for his name and for all his people assembled through him, even if they never be refreshed by the clear and boundless waters that flow from beneath the temple.

Leo Tolstoy was fond of a particular Russian folk story of God's forgiveness, which he included in his long novel *War and Peace.*

Several Russian prisoners are telling the tale of their crimes that put them in Siberia. An old man relates that he was innocent, but unable to overcome the circumstantial evidence. Another prisoner listening to his words admits that he was the guilty one who committed that particular murder many years ago. Efforts are then made through official channels to win the innocent old man's release.

> So he [the murderer] confessed and it was all written down and the papers sent off in due form. The place was a long way off, and while they were judging, what with one thing and another, filling in the papers all in due form—the authorities I mean—time passed. The affair reached the Tsar. After a while the Tsar's decree came: to set the merchant free and give him a compensation that had been awarded. The paper arrived and they began to look for the old man. "Where is the old man who has been suffering innocently and in vain? A paper has come from the Tsar!" So they began looking for him . . . but God had already forgiven him—he was dead![4]

In this story humanity suffers from the sins of the whole world, and death is a full pardon and restoration from the Lord of the universe.

In the Gospels, the quintessential story of God's forgiveness remains the parable of the "Prodigal Son" in the fifteenth chapter of Luke. Having given his younger son his share of the inheritance, which was the father's income and security in his old age, the father daily goes to the top of the hill to gaze at the distant horizon for the first sign of his son's homecoming. When he finally notices him a long way off, he runs to greet his son and falls upon his neck in a welcoming embrace. The son's bitter self-accusation for his sins and ingratitude does not affect the father's heartfelt greeting. He cares not for past sins; he cares only for this son of his who was lost and now is found. "Quickly bring the finest robe and put it on him; put a ring on his finger and sandals on his feet." Surely it would seem to be the father who is prodigal in his love, a spendthrift of mercy and forgiveness who can withhold nothing from his beloved son. We believe the judge of this world is this same father, the Abba-father of our Lord Jesus Christ. Rightly then Christians believe in the "forgiveness of sins."

The culmination of belief in the Father Almighty, Jesus Christ his Son, and the Holy Spirit, who animates the church in its daily interdependent communal life, has been reached at the end of this eleventh article of the creed. What Christians believe about sinfulness amounts to this. Sin is an offense against God. Sin is not merely a disruption of the created order; at bottom it is a refusal of God's self-gift. Similarly, forgiveness of sin is not the therapeutic agency of God who maintains the world; it is the uncreated gift of God's self. "Receive the holy Spirit. Whose sins you forgive are forgiven them, and whose sins you retain are retained" (John 20:22–23). After the crucifixion of Jesus, he returns to those who abandoned him and breaks bread with them in reconciliation. In that bread Jesus gives himself, his body and his blood. Salvation is ever God's self-gift, and forgiveness is equally God's self-gift. In the creed we deal with the uncreated mystery of God, and not just the manifestations of his power in the created order. The "forgiveness of sins" sums up the amazing extent of God's love and God's infinite being, which is never just gift, but ever self-gift.

That our sins are forgiven once and for all is a way of saying God is truly for us. If the infinite God is for us, who can be against us? St. Paul promises this:

> If God is for us, who can be against us? He who did not spare his own Son but handed him over for us all, how will he not also give us everything else along with him? Who will bring a charge against God's chosen ones? It is God who acquits us. Who will condemn? It is Christ [Jesus] who died, rather, was raised, who also is at the right hand of God, who indeed intercedes for us. What will separate us from the love of Christ? (Rom. 8:31–35)

We are the beloved. The gates of hell will not prevail against this community. The last articles of the creed simply make manifest what being so chosen entails. "Forgiveness of sins" leads to "resurrection of the body and life everlasting" with the God who loved us first and last, despite (even because of) our sinfulness.

EPILOGUE

Lord of Salvation

The eleventh article of the creed declares that the greatest work of creation remains the conversion of the human heart. The Spirit of God is Lord of salvation. The Spirit of God can melt the human heart, soften its resistance, and bring it forgiveness of sins. The reconciliation of enemies is a greater creation than to bring something out of nothing, for here God must first undo the evil, then move within human freedom, and finally bring about communion from a poisoned well. That God writes straight with crooked lines is a sign of God's unsurpassable lordship.

What follows for us is this. The grace of God is loose in the world, and the Holy Spirit through grace-filled events seeks to transform us and transfigure our lives. The encounter with grace may be a break-through that comes from angry conflict, sexual passion, illness or accident, a book that challenges, or a decision taken alone in conscience. We all encounter such transcendent invitations, although not every day. They tend to punctuate our lives. It is then we are invited to step outside of loving only our own self-service and self-interest. It is then we are invited to commit ourselves somehow to the good embodied in other human beings. Our promises become our bond. What we then do is to take a stand for eternity rather than just for time, for God rather than just for ourselves. Thus are our sins forgiven.

ARTICLE XII

To TURN TO THE twelfth article: "the resurrection of the body, and the life everlasting." The immediate insight sees the restoration of the body and life without end. Our imagination can hardly transcend the state of the body as we know it. The resurrection of the body may seem just more of what we know here and now. Life eternal may easily seem an endless succession of our days.

The further insight sees the resurrection of the body and life eternal as the expansion of space (body) and time (life). Begun in the Spirit even here in this earthly life, the life to come will transfigure space and time. We will be born again into a new heaven and a new earth. A qualitative leap is envisioned, more than just a quantitative one. Nor will this life and its history be left behind in the world to come. The scars and wounds of this life will be linked to our happiness. Jesus showed his glorified wounds to doubting Thomas. The immortal life to come keeps touch with this mortal life. The creed ends with an appeal to glory as only God knows glory. The body will transcend space in glory, and time will become our perduring relationship with God. Always (time) and everywhere (space) it is right and fitting to give thanks to God.

Carnis Resurrectionem

The Latin "carnis resurrectionem" means "the resurrection of the body." The Latin would support a more literal translation, that is, "resurrection of the flesh." One might think of English usage such as "all flesh shall see the salvation of God" (Luke 3:6). The distinction is subtle. Whatever the translation, the last article of the creed promises humanity that same resurrection that raised Jesus from the dead on the third day. Because humanity has been given the Holy Spirit that proceeds from the Father and Son, it is given to hope that the church of all humanity in the communion of saints will find its past wounds healed for the forgiveness of sins that leads to the resurrection of the body and future life without end. Paul writes: "If the Spirit of the one who raised Jesus from the dead dwells in you, the one who raised Christ from the dead will give life to your mortal bodies also, through his Spirit that dwells in you" (Rom. 8:11). The space and time world of the church on earth, even now filled with the Spirit of God, will then intersect with eternity. The body which exists in space will know "eternal space," or the condition of a resurrected body; the body which exists in time will know "eternal time," or the condition of a life everlasting, world without end.

Just as the communion of saints makes possible the forgiveness of sins, so the forgiveness of sins prepares the resurrection of the body. St. Paul says "the wages of sin is death" (Rom. 6:23). When sins are forgiven and division overcome in the communion of holy people, the body lives and death itself is overcome. The wages of grace is life. This forgiveness takes place in the church, in the community that loves one another, in the body which continues to sin, but now is incorporated into the body of Christ whose blood was shed for many for the forgiveness of sins. When Jesus who was crucified came back to sinners and broke bread with them again, they knew they were forgiven. That bread of reconciliation could only mean the risen Lord's bond, the pledge of the resurrection of the body so valued by the Lord of life. God's love is persevering love. God's love is on-going conversation and a never-ending relationship. Life everlasting means the dance goes on. Given the love of God for us, body and soul, our body cannot be thrown down in death. "He will not allow his beloved to see corruption" (Ps. 16:10). When the past is reconciled to God, the future is incorporated in the body of the church and its members who will rise in glory to the "resurrection of the body and life everlasting."

The Christian creed does not put forward for belief the doctrine of "the immortality of the soul." Not that Christians dispute the doctrine of the soul that perdures beyond the dissolution of the body, especially when that doctrine is understood not as a questionable human anthropology, but rather as a theological defense of the individual after death. The creed says nothing of the soul. It affirms simply that the body shall arise from death. The Hebrew scriptures have no tradition of a happy human condition where soul and body are separate. Hebrew thought saw a human being as an animated body, a living thing, where soul and body conjointly make the human being. It is more the Greek world of philosophy that saw the soul as the seat of thought and spirit, a non-material being, capable of surviving the death of the body, and in some ways dependent for its very freedom upon transcending the imprisonment of the body in this life.

Neither Hebrew nor Greek stand fully content with the philosophical separation of soul and body. Aristotelian philosophy speaks of the body and soul as distinct entities, but not separate ones. A human being was not the addition of a soul to a body existing as a human body without it. Union of body and soul was more intimate and co-constitutive than that. Body and soul might be distinct, but never separate. Their union was mysterious. Nevertheless, experience demonstrated the dissolution of the body in death, and inner conviction wished to maintain that a human being outlives death. In face of the corpse at hand, both Hebrew and Greek thought reluctantly concluded that half a loaf was better than none at all. The immortality of the soul was better than annihilation. Although some philosophers might contend that an unencumbered soul enjoyed a superior condition after death, the bulk of humanity did not find such a condition very enviable. A ghostly experience could not even be imagined; human beings were not bodiless spirits, nor was an angelic condition a human way of life. Poets of the ancient world imagined the realm of the dead as an underworld. In the Hebrew *Sheol* and in the Greek *Hades* the dead experienced a thin and bloodless condition. They were "shades" with their body reduced to its shadow, which once the vital and active body cast as its insubstantial image. The shade, or shadowy body, was a compromise, a stab in the dark, a speculation about life after death as it could be imagined.

When Odysseus descends to the underworld, he gives to the dead a bowl of blood to drink to replenish their bodily vitality. Only in this way would they have the energy to speak a few words to him. Their bodily condition is bleak and attenuated. The English poet Andrew

Marvell captures the mood: "The grave's a fine and private place, /
But none I think do there embrace."[1] Homer has Achilles lament that
he would rather be a slave on earth than a king there below. Given
a choice between long life without fame and death in battle glorious,
Achilles had chosen death, which now he bitterly regrets.

The Old Testament writers had no elaborate and clear belief in
resurrection, although they held there was life, greatly diminished,
no doubt, after death. They may have thought of Sheol much as the
neighboring pagans did. They may have had an implicit faith that the
transcendent God of creation would not let the gift of a human life
fall into total oblivion. In the time of Jesus, the Sadducees were the
more conservative party that accepted only the Torah as their rule
of faith. They found no doctrine of the resurrection of the body in
the first five books of the Hebrew Bible. Hence they came to Jesus
with their smug conundrum: If there were a resurrection of the body,
how would one provide for the woman who had sequentially married
seven husbands? Whose wife would she be in a bodily afterworld?
(Mark 12:19–23)

The Pharisees and other Jewish groups contemporary with Jesus did believe in some kind of resurrection. They took consolation
from the martyrdom of the seven sons in the Second Book of Mac-
cabees (and from the Book of Daniel, chapters 7 and 12). The argument of such a position revolves around God's creation, which cannot be in vain. The God who created the body can re-create a body
for those who loved God and who gave up their body for their faith.
The mother of the seven sons says: "I do not know how you came
into being in my womb. It was not I who gave you life and breath,
nor I who set in order the elements within each of you. Therefore,
the Creator of the world, who shaped the beginning of man and devised
the origin of all things, will in his mercy give life and breath back
to you again, since you did not forget yourselves for the sake of his
laws" (7:22–23). In some sense, the resurrection of the body is hidden
in the deepest implications of the creation of the body by an eternally
faithful and almighty God, who seeks an on-going relationship with
humankind.

One might ask whether or not Christians actually believe more
in the salvation of the soul or in the resurrection of the body? Christians believe in the transfiguration of the whole human being, body
and soul. If they talk of the "salvation of souls," they may be thinking
with Greek imagination, but they are affirming in faith the resurrection victory. If they talk of the "resurrection of the body," they may

be thinking with Hebrew imagination, but they are affirming in faith resurrection unto eternal and transcendent life. Indeed, one might argue that in Christianity immortality and resurrection converge.

After death, it may be asked, do Christians believe a human being has a body? Do they await the resurrection of the body only on the last day? In the meantime, are human beings naked ghosts without their bodies? Between the particular judgment and the last (general) judgment is there a bodiless interregnum? The Nicene Creed speaks of the "resurrection of the *dead*," whereas the Apostles' Creed more precisely promises the "resurrection of the *body*." That translation of the Latin "carnis" dates from the time of the English Reformation. Previously the text had been rendered "resurrection of the *flesh*" or the "uprising of the flesh." The Latin "*carnis* resurrectionem" and the Greek equivalent "*sarkos* anastasis" would very literally support such earlier translations. One might argue that the resurrection of the body (and even more so "of the dead") could be interpreted as belief in some form of survival of the body-person, but not necessarily an individual survival. Some form of transmigration of souls could claim resurrection of the body, and proclaim that no spiritual life actually dies. Yet the Christian kerygma is still more radical. This body of this human being, this flesh, will rise. Even this claim must not be taken so literally that an exact molecular restructuring of the body is imagined. Nonetheless, the belief remains that the individual with their own flesh and their own particular history will live. How so?

Christians believe that there is an immediate and particular judgment (or judging revelation) at death, and there remains a last and general judgment at the end of time. Then all human history will be justified; then judgment will be complete. Let us suggest that there must be some form of resurrection of the body at death and judgment for each individual. It is clear that there must be an interim state between the individual's death and the final coming of Christ. It remains implausible to argue for an immediate and final resurrection of the body, unless perhaps one argues for an interim state that suffers no passing time but stands in an eternal now. It would seem more understandable to argue either for a disembodied condition for the interim, or to argue for an intermediate resurrection of the body. Ladislaus Boros speaks of the end of time as "the final completion of the resurrection that had already occurred at death. . . . This would mean that the human soul is never without a body; immortality and resurrection are in fact one and the same."[2] Fortman concludes from his survey of theologians writing on this matter:

That the precise nature of my "risen body" is still wrapped in deep mystery. But the "I" of my pilgrim life, will continue through my interim life and on through my final life. And this "I," this person that I am, will not be just a disembodied consciousness, soul or spirit. "I" will have an "interim embodiment" in the interim state, and a final embodiment in the final state, that will fit me for my interim and final existence and activity. Beyond this we are surrounded by mystery.[3]

Fullness of the resurrection of the body awaits the full communion of the saints in the parousia when the Kingdom has finally come. Only then will the entire social solidarity and interdependence of our bodily lives, that are immersed in all the ages of human history and human intentions, be transfigured. Only in that Second Coming, that general judgment, that general "revelation," will the fullness of the resurrection of the body reside. General judgment and general resurrection of the body will converge. But, just as eternal life begins now and culminates then, so resurrection of the body begins now, is sustained through death, and is completed when the Kingdom of God has come on earth as in heaven. John, who so often would have the kingdom now, has Jesus say: "I am the resurrection and the life" (11: 25), and even in this world "I am the way and the truth and the life" (14:6).

Our difficulty with resurrection of the body *now* and also *then* stems from our inability to image eternity without the parameters of time, where we can recognize a before and an after, a now and a then. We await the endtime; God already knows the endtime. The dead who are in the hands of God share this perspective of eternity. They do not await the endtime as we do. The Kingdom of God in this world has yet to fulfill its time, but the Kingdom in eternity remains beyond time as we know it. The resurrection of the body, therefore, need not be understood as something the blessed in heaven await to happen to them in this our earthly time.

Even with such an affirmation of eternity, the Christian hope of resurrection does not abandon time in favor of embracing only eternity. This world and this our body remain the beginning of eternal life, and we take with us after death not just a body, but our body. Resurrection may re-create and transfigure our body beyond imagination, but our body nonetheless. My body is so much my matter; the body is relentlessly private. Love in the body becomes exclusive because one cannot be in two beds at once. Rape and physical abuse strike such devastation in the individual because such violence tends to denigrate identification with the body, denying that it truly belongs to the person who suffers it. Death thus threatens to take away all that is mine, and that only which is mine. Simone Weil says that the desire to make love to a human being inevitably hides a hunger for the incarnation, that is, a desire to hold the infinite in one's bodily arms. In his play, *Partage de Midi*,[4] Paul Claudel has the heroine, Ysè, who represents a forbidden love, proclaim to the hero of the drama: "I am not God, but God made me." So often the body and its attachments become "the promise that cannot be held" of the God who awaits us.

Somehow we believe that God will gather us up; that reunion will be the resurrection of the body. Our earthly condition and our bodily existence will not prove the first stage of a lift-off into an eternal orbit, the booster body being negligible and programmed to disintegrate in its fall back to the ground. Our body is to be transfigured, not jettisoned. We will gather up our body. Our activity and our history, the merits of our virtues and the forgiveness of our sins for the deeds we did while in the body, will not be lost. In the resurrection appearances, Jesus can be recognized by those who loved him as Jesus of Nazareth. He can talk and eat, and yet he comes and goes as if he can be in two places at once. His glorious wounds identify him as the crucified Jesus, only now his sufferings are worn like jewels of glory. We recognize our body by its perduring scars, by its unique fingerprint ridges in our flesh. Death shall not obliterate nor undo the past. Our bonds and relationships will not be in vain. Death and resurrection will fulfill the past, preserve our history unto glory, fulfill yesterday in the ongoing life of tomorrow. Such is the Christian hope.

Just as there is no heaven on earth in this vale of tears, so there is no earthly paradise in heaven. Although in the resurrection of the body death will be no more and "God will wipe away every tear" (Rev. 7:17), Christians expect more than just the good things of this life without lack or interruption. Heaven is to be "a new heaven and a new earth" (Rev. 21:1). The resurrected body is a new body, a transfigured body, a body lifted to eternal glory before the face of God. Will there be heavenly food and a new kind of touch in the body? Will our friendships and loves endure and blossom? Will we hear heavenly music and look upon the wonders of our God? Food and sex, so much a part of the pleasures of this earthly life, will not be needed for earthly reasons. We will not need food to keep ourselves alive, nor sex to keep the human race alive. If practical needs disappear, what will the body enjoy? One could imagine a variety of transcendent de-

lights. Aquinas in his commentary on this article of the creed specu-
lates that we shall all be about thirty-three years of age, with a body
that enjoys incorruptibility. That human body will be brilliant, im-
passible, agile (think of the human body in space), and subtle or transparent.[6] Fortman, commenting on these traditional qualities, writes:

> In virtue of its impassibility the risen body would be immortal
> and no longer susceptible of suffering, sickness, death or any
> bodily evil whatever. It would be immune to pain, frailty, hun-
> ger, thirst, weariness, exhaustion. It would have no need to eat,
> drink, or sleep. By its splendor the risen body would "shine as
> the sun" (Mt. 13:43). It would have perfect bodily beauty and its
> own special light which could be suspended by the blessed at
> will. The radiance of the soul would irradiate the body as light
> within it irradiates a crystal. Subtility would make the risen body
> perfectly docile to the spirit and give it a share in many of the
> powers and privileges of the spirit. Very likely it would give it
> the power to compenetrate other bodies. By its agility the risen
> body of the blessed would be able to move easily from place to
> place, perhaps from planet to planet, from star to star, with the
> speed of thought. And thus the wide expanse of the universe,
> the remotest recesses of the starry skies would be accessible to
> the risen bodies of the blessed.[7]

What a transfiguration of the body and its functions in this practical earthly life might be like we cannot know in detail. We know
we shall not in any way be disappointed nor lack the genuine fulfillment of human bodily nature swept up into the mystery of God. The
bodily satisfactions of this life will be enhanced and quite transfigured. Therefore, to the question will heaven be infinitely new and
varied, never exhausted, never lacking anything, Christians say "yes"
and then more. "What eye has not seen, and ear has not heard, and
what has not entered the human heart, what God has prepared for
those who love him" (1 Cor. 2:9). And Jesus says in St. John's gospel:
"In my Father's house there are many dwelling places. If there were
not, would I have told you that I am going to prepare a place for you?"
(14:2). We shall indeed behold God, and in God we shall hold each
other more intimately and profoundly than we ever did in the body
of this world, whose contacts were necessarily but on the surface of
the skin. "At present we see indistinctly, as in a mirror, but then face
to face" (1 Cor. 13:12).

But how can all this be? How do we even imagine a world beyond our experience, yet inclusive and respectful of it? Who would

have thought the oak tree would issue from the acorn? Or the rose come forth from the dung? Paul writes: "So also is the resurrection of the dead. It is sown corruptible; it is raised incorruptible. It is sown dishonorable; it is raised glorious. It is sown weak; it is raised powerful. It is sown a natural body; it is raised a spiritual·body. If there is a natural body, there is also a spiritual one" (1 Cor. 15:42–44). Who would have imagined that the worm would turn, and that from the cocoon of an earlier life should emerge a dazzle-colored butterfly that flies instead of crawls? Who would think that a raindrop could suddenly produce a rainbow of every color, or a sunset be revealed from gray clouds moments before? Who has seen a peacock suddenly fan out its tail that was dragging in the barnyard muck and not be breathless that such a lavish beauty could appear so suddenly and from such an unpromising scene. Flannery O'Connor wrote: "Christ will come like that."[8]

Who would have thought that from the egg we should find a live chick coming out from its broken shell? The colored eggs of Eastertide, hidden in the grass, are childish images and homely images, no doubt, of how the Lord of life burst the limits of the tomb and threw back the heavy stone that trapped human hope in the dark grave. Who can explain to the unborn child in its mother's womb what it would be like to fall in love, to marry and bear a child, to dance wildly and to think deep thoughts, to grow wise and to worship the infinite God, who took flesh in a womb just as we all have done. Birth must be such an adventure for the unborn, such a shock, such an unimaginable new world for the infant who has yet to breathe with its own lungs this air of an utterly new world. And we, we are born into eternal life, now to die no more. "In him we live and move and have our being" (Acts 17:28).

(Et) Vitam Aeternam

The Latin "(et) vitam aeternam" means "(and) in eternal life." Some English translations prefer to render the text "(and) in life everlasting." The creed closes with this proclamation of perduring life. The Old Roman Creed did not include this phrase, which was gradually incorporated in the established text. The Nicene Creed does confess belief in "the life of the world to come." The advent of the Kingdom of God was thought to be the long-awaited and final age. Then would be the eternal age when God reigned, and the aeon without end would be without blemish. Both creeds affirm this kingdom without end. Both phrases are found in several places in the Bible. "Amen, amen, I say to you, whoever hears my word and believes in the one who sent me has eternal life and will not come to condemnation, but has passed from death to life" (John 5:24). In Matthew's judgment scene, the blessed are invited to enter into "eternal life" (25:46). And Matthew speaking of sins against the Holy Spirit says that they "will not be forgiven, either in this age or in the age to come" (12:32). It may seem the Apostles' Creed chooses a more quantative metaphor, "*eternal* life," whereas the Nicene Creed presents a more qualitative metaphor, "life *in the age to come*". The Kingdom of God, of course, enjoys in a preeminent way the fullness of both quantity and quality.

Examples of the creed with the conjunction "and" (*et* in Latin) preceding the last phrase of the creed can frequently be found. J. N. D. Kelly gives the established text (Textus Receptus) of the Apostles' Creed as *et vitam aeternam*. Kelly follows the *Ordo Romanus Antiquus*, which he describes as a document "authoritative in the West in the later middle ages, and which the reformers themselves adopted as their norm—except that Luther read *Christian* for *Catholic*."[9] In his *Enchiridion* (paragraphs 84 and 108), Augustine uses the preposition "*in* vitam aeternam," which is usually rendered in English "resurrection of the body *unto* life everlasting." The significance of this perhaps trivial matter lies in this. Are we justified in yoking "resurrection of the body *and* life eternal" to make the last article of the creed? Or, do we have two disjunctive articles, whose meanings may appropriately diverge? We know "eternal life" was a late-established addition to the Old Roman Creed. With or without the conjunction in the established text, I have chosen to conjoin "resurrection of the body and life eternal." The matter, however, does not yield a simple and certain resolution.

This final phrase of the Apostles' Creed adds little that is not implied in the "resurrection of the body," or even in the confession of "his kingdom will never end" that concludes the second part of the creed in the Nicene formulation. The creed might have been expressed as the "resurrection of time and the body that lives" and still have said much the same thing. God is Lord of space (the resurrected body) and equally Lord of time (eternal life). Humankind is not lord of time. Gerhard Ebeling writes:

> He wants to be lord over his time, and this makes him ever more subject to it.
>
> God is the Lord of time. Eternity is his divine power over time, the unlimited freedom to apportion time and to end it.

Eternity and time are not disparate entities that cancel one another; at a profound level they are complementary. Time is the utterance of eternity; eternity is the mystery of time. They belong together like creator and creation. This means that the intelligibility of eternity embraces two elements: the divinity of God and the humanity of man.[10]

The life of the world to come is life eternal, because Jesus Christ's kingdom will never end. Life will not be overcome; death shall now be no more. If it were ever possible to read the resurrection of the body to mean a resuscitation of the dead in the manner of Lazarus who would in time die again, this last phrase of the creed insists upon an ampler belief in eternal life in a world without end.

Such an eternal world is surely heaven. Yet, heaven is not the discovery of the fountain of youth to keep us from aging, nor an immortality under conditions of this life which do not preserve us from the ravages of time. Longevity is not eternity. Odysseus found immortality with the beautiful goddess, Calypso, boring. Only the prospect of death brings a piquant flavor to the endless passage of time, which otherwise postpones definitive decision indefinitely. Heaven is neither an arrested moment of this sweet life, nor an ageless succession of moments of this world's time. We can neither bring about heaven on earth, as Marx hoped, nor bring about earth in heaven, as Mohammed hoped. Nevertheless, it is not true to speak of a split between earth and heaven, between time and eternity. Rather, eternal life begins in time and is fulfilled in eternity. The fellowship and communion with God begun in this life with the indwelling of the Holy Spirit goes on, but then without the concealing veil. John says: "We shall see him as he is" (1 John 3:2). In this life now we see God by the light of faith; then we shall see the Light itself without need for faith. Love will perdure, and in love we will be united to God without the medium of creation, which is now our condition, even though in the gift of the Holy Spirit we have even now a foretaste of eternal life. Jesus says: "I am the resurrection and the life; whoever believes in me, even if he die, will live, and everyone who lives and believes in me will never die" (John 11:25–26).

When heaven is thought of as the knowledge and love of God beyond this life, yet now begun in this life, heaven and earth are not so separated. The Christian creed does not denigrate this life in order to enhance the value of the life to come. Such an attitude can use heaven to excuse men and women from the tasks of justice and love on this earth. Such an attitude can trash the earth and consider it only as a disposable arena in which the soul gains its victory. Marx called such a promised heaven "the opium of the people." The ideology of an oppressive ruling class will not grant justice for all on earth but is willing to point to heaven. Conversely, the creed does not lower heaven in order to elevate this earth. Dylan Thomas' poem, "Do not go gentle into that good night,"[11] reminds us how readily we cling to this life, the only sweetness we can touch. How reluctant we are to abandon ourselves to the mystery of death, even if it be found within the mystery of God.

We want to love this life and the life to come, precisely because the good in both stems from God. Love life now and live life now, because all life comes from God, remains with God, and whenever genuinely treasured leads to God. The crucified and risen Lord is the way, the truth, and the life. Christians must follow Christ in this life, in order to be with him in the next. Jesus is their way of life now, and not just a guarantor of a better life then. And yet, Jesus was crucified and died. Let the poor of the earth take some consolation that no servant is greater than their master. "For if we have grown into union with him through a death like his, we shall also be united with him in the resurrection" (Rom. 6:5).

The Christian glimpses eternal life whenever there is an experience of grace in this life, for it is the gratuitous intervention of God that opens a window upon eternity. In such moments we transcend this world of time and dying. We break into eternal life, and one instance of such an open horizon can outweigh years of discouragement. Moments of grace occur in some association with the transcendentals, such as goodness (and justice), truth, beauty, and oneness. When we experience these moments of eternity in a transparent way, we recognize that only the infinite God could validate and sustain them. For example, the person who knows that the good must be done as an imperative, and that deliberately turning from the good is the greatest evil, suddenly knows God in eternity. Both Socrates and Jesus go to their death for transcendent reasons. Persons who stand for the truth when it is not expedient risk their lives, only because they know that truth upholds their life, and to lose the truth is worse than to be dead. The person who glimpses the face of God in a moment of beauty unveiled knows that there are tears, both of joy and of sorrow, too deep for words. The person who, in the spirit of the beatitudes that urge transcendence upon us, hungers for justice and takes a stand in its favor has been promised eternal life in God. Persons who hunger to be at one with God and humankind, who forgive seven times seven, who count not the cost of love, do so because they know such love is boundless and stems from the eternal love of God. In moments of grace, a transcendent love has laid hold of them with the promise of eternal life.

It is in these moments of grace, when we transcend the world and take a decision for eternity, that we decide what our attitude toward God shall truly be. We become in time our eternal self. We make with provisional decisions over the course of a lifetime the definitive "yes" or "no" to God that is eternal life, either heaven or hell. How terrible it would be if time were endless, if our choices were never-ending, if the portrait of ourselves we worked upon so long and claim as a true likeness were always to fade away. It would be no blessing never to die to time and change. The blessing is to enter eternity, so that the who and the what we have come to treasure becomes finally irrevocable, where neither moth consumes nor thief robs. Tentative life without outcome forever would be unbearable. The reader may recall the early days of the Polaroid camera. Unless the photo was fixed by brushing a special chemical over its surface, the images would gradually fade in a matter of days. It is death that fixes our decisions, so that when we have them just right, we may hold them for life everlasting and not lose them to one more unneeded and unwanted revision. We shall enter eternal life thus as our best self.

One might ask, what happens in "eternal life"? Whatever it may be, such life in heaven is thinkable only in our present space-time images. We can try to speak of the New Jerusalem (see Rev. 21), or we can fall silent. We usually claim that heaven is ineffable, as much mystery as God. We frequently take the *via negativa* and argue that heaven transcends everything we know of this earth. And yet, can we not affirm some general truths about heaven and eternal life?

The essence of heaven remains the sight of God. "We shall see him as he is" (1 John 3:2). Now we see "as in a mirror, but then face to face" (1 Cor. 13:12). We shall see God. We shall see God not reflected in created things that mirror his glory, as we see objects in this world reflected in the light of the sun. We shall look directly into the sun. We shall look upon the light, and not the reflection of the light. We shall see God face to face, without a veil, without a medium of communication, naked and without barrier. Our knowledge and love for God then will not be derivative of this world, but wholly the result of the divine favor and grace. In the light of glory (lumen gloriae) we shall see light itself. We shall look upon the face of God and live. In that sight of God in all of God's mystery and infinite goodness and beauty we shall be made happy beyond all measure. Our happiness will cascade into ever future rapture as the inexhaustible and infinite God is ever more disclosed. In that beatific vision we shall see God fully revealed, as God is, face to face without sacrament or faith, knowing God as God knows God, Father and Son and Holy Spirit, to the full extent that a creature with the grace of God can be elevated into the life and bliss of the ineffable God.

Let us assert that heaven will be the best that an infinitely resourceful God can provide. Eternal life will be happiness-producing and boundlessly engaging. It will never be boring, insecure, sinful, lacking, or temporary. If sitting on a cloud or playing a harp images heaven, those moments will be infinitely more than our cartoon versions of heaven as a vacuous place where nothing happens and there is no excitement. If God is bored or deprived, or misses out on earthly sensual life, then so will we. If God loses out because there is no change and development in God's life, then so will we. If God does not comprehend that the medium is part of the message and the trip part of the joy of the destination, then we will share this deprivation. However, if God is infinitely alive, dynamic and yet restful, everything that can ever be all at once, then so will we be fulfilled to the extent that a creature can be filled with the being of the Creator. Moreover, our happiness will be communal and social; we shall know and love one another in the communion of the saints. And finally, we shall gather around God and enjoy God's life in a human bodily way, precisely because we shall all be centered around Jesus Christ our Lord, whose Kingdom will never end.

Quite simply put, the essence of heaven is union with God. The satiety and fullness of heaven will confirm that God alone suffices, for in God eminently resides all the good that we have been so attracted to in its diffused and reflected condition in the created world. Just as white light eminently contains the rainbow, and just as the ballerina eminently can walk like a girl and crawl like an infant, so God contains supremely all that could delight us with its goodness. In the infinite Being, all being that is created as not-God is yet nestled in God in the inexhaustible mystery of the One and the Many. All being participates in the bountiful God. "In his light we see light" (Ps. 36:9).

The metaphors of the Kingdom in the Old and New Testaments give us some idea of the richness of heaven, a richness that does not suggest the evacuation of the good things of this earth. In Isaiah we read: "For behold, I create new heavens and a new earth; and the former things shall not be remembered or come to mind" (65:17). Revelation echoes this passage: "Then I saw a new heaven and a new earth. The former heaven and the former earth had passed away, and the sea was no more. I also saw the holy city, a new Jerusalem, coming down out of heaven from God, prepared as a bride adorned for her husband" (21:1–2). Matthew describes eternal life in heaven with the metaphor of a "wedding feast" (25:10). Luke speaks of "eternal dwellings" (16:9), and Paul talks of wearing an "imperishable crown" (1 Cor. 9:25) and going "home to the Lord" (2 Cor. 5:7). The heavenly banquet, the ever-flowing fountain, the flourishing tree, the light that never dims, the justice that triumphs, the ultimate freedom, the consummate love, these are the earthly metaphors of heaven. Always the images suggest an earth not to be abandoned, but an earth to be transfigured unto eternal life. "Amen, I say to you, today you will be with me in Paradise" (Luke 23:43). And Paul writes:

> We know that all creation is groaning in labor pains even until now; and not only that, but we ourselves, who have the first-fruits of the Spirit, we also groan within ourselves as we wait for adoption, the redemption of our bodies. For in hope we were saved. Now hope that sees for itself is not hope. For who hopes for what one sees? But if we hope for what we do not see, we wait with endurance. (Rom. 8:22–25)

To believe in "eternal life" is but another way to believe in God. Jesus is Lord does indeed say it all. The various articles of the creed reduce themselves to variations on this theme.

EPILOGUE

Lord of Space and Time

The twelfth article of the creed declares that God is Lord of the body in space (resurrection of the body) and Lord of the body in time (life eternal). God is Lord of space and time. God is Lord of created matter, which exists only in space, and whose motion, when measured, defines times. God is Lord of motion, of change, of becoming as well as being. Space and time will be brought to fulfillment in God's eternity.

For us what follows in this. God's eternity is the goal of all of our earthly space and time adventure. The resurrected body is the body transfigured beyond space parameters; life eternal is the world transfigured beyond the limits of time that adds more only by taking away what has been. The present moment will give way to the eternal moment. Our being will finally be perfected and perdure. Becoming will be fulfilled in full being. The world will no longer need to change for the better, for the best will be assured. The world of space and time with all the "slings and arrows of outrageous fortune" will be brought before God and securely transfigured there forever, where the wounds of this life, made glorious, shall shine like the sun. "In him we live and move and have our being" (Acts 17:28).

Summary of Part One of the Apostles' Creed

The creed is divided into three parts, corresponding to the three persons in the Trinity. Part one deals with God who is Father-Almighty. Adequately understood, to affirm the existence of God worthy of the name yields the mystery of an infinite and sovereign God beyond our imagination and our reason, both origin and end of all that exists. Many times the popular understanding of God reduces God to our logical mind. We conceive of God as one being among many, as one power among many forces, although we concede God is the greatest being and the largest power. That theology falls short of the infinite God, as a million zeros fall short of an infinite number. God is everything, and yet creation is not God. God is the infinite One, and yet the Many are not God. God does everything, and yet our freedom remains genuine. This mystery of the One and the Many, this mystery of the infinite and sovereign God ought to come to the reader as a shock. God ever remains an enormous contradiction to our minds. To make God only one factor among many in the world is to settle for a demi-God, who is finally no God. Conversely, to make God the only factor in the world is finally to settle for our own non-existence. We must hold to both sides of this paradoxical mystery equally. We must let God be God, and nonetheless we must be ourselves.

In explaining part one of the creed, I have not tried to prove the existence of God. From one point of view the very effort begins in illusion, for it assumes that we can begin from a standpoint that does not already presume God, upon whom we depend in order to investigate the existence of God. One might not want to give this ground away so easily. Great thinkers in the Western tradition have tried to prove the existence of God. Aristotle arguing from a prime mover, Anselm from the nature of perfection, Aquinas from casuality, Descartes from intuition, Pascal from a wager on eternity, and Kant from a moral imperative come to mind as classic expositions. The church has never canonized any one of these arguments, although the first Vatican Council defends the capacity of human reason to prove the

159

existence of God, regardless of whether or not anyone has actually done so, or who such a person might be.

Having presupposed the existence of God, I wish now to claim what a difference the existence of God makes to the believer. The question of God is a question of all or nothing. If there is a God, the world is a gift for which we should give thanks always and everywhere. If there is no God, the world is finally absurd and we have no one but ourselves. We wish often a middle position, not so stark as outlined above. We want the benefits of the existence of God without the explicit rhetoric and religious fervor it sets off. But there is no middle position. Most people who find meaning and goodness in life piggy-back on the theist position, whether they consciously acknowledge it or not. Cardinal Newman argued for a place for theology, the study of God, in university education. So many of the brightest minds over the centuries have testified to the importance of the question of God. Newman insisted that if by such inquiry anything were indeed known about God, then the implications were enormous. He writes:

> With us Catholics, as with the first race of Protestants, as with Mahometans, and all Theists, the word [God] contains, as I have already said, a theology in itself. . . . According to the teaching of Monotheism, God is an Individual, Self-dependent, All-perfect, Unchangeable Being; intelligent, living, personal, and present; almighty, all-seeing, all-remembering; between whom and His creatures there is an infinite gulf; who has no origin, who is all-sufficient for Himself; who created and upholds the universe; who will judge every one of us, sooner or later, according to the Law of right and wrong which He has written on our hearts. He is One who is sovereign over, operative amidst, independent of, the appointments which He has made; One in whose hands are all things, who has a purpose in every event, and a standard for every deed, and thus has relations of His own towards the subject-matter of each particular science which the book of knowledge unfolds; who has with an adorable, never-ceasing energy implicated Himself in all the history of creation, the constitution of nature, the course of the world, the origin of society, the fortunes of nations, the action of the human mind; and who thereby necessarily becomes the subject-matter of a science, far wider and more noble than any of those which are included in the circle of secular Education.[1]

To oversimplify, there is no other question but God. Everything depends upon it. "If God is for us, who can be against us?" And similarly, if there is no infinite God, that is in effect if "God" is against us, who can be for us? Theology goes on to unfold the word God in many volumes. All of them are commentary. The creed settles for a short sentence of explanation. The contemporary world indeed acknowledges the question of God, but does not always keep the religious language in which it has traditionally been raised. Dag Hammarskjold talks of a "yes or no" to life in his journal, *Markings,* and Martin Buber tells of a "Thou" that saves us from solipsism. Whether it is God or Godot we are waiting for, my intention in this commentary on the first part has been achieved if the reader grasps that what is at stake is everything or nothing, light or darkness, life or death.

Finally, this first part should not be construed as exclusively a statement about God. That God exists is not a piece of interesting information about another world for the curious in this world. Knowledge about God is knowledge about ourselves. We are brothers and sisters only if God is Father. We are upheld in a loving providence that sustains creation in an on-going way, guiding all events large and small wisely and well, only if God is Almighty. We are creatures of God and gifts from God, only if God is creator. That we are depends ultimately on that God is. What we are depends on what God is. That we can know the truth or love the good, not skeptically but authentically, depends on the validation provided for such transcendence by the existence of God-Father-Almighty. There would remain no "us" to believe anything unless there is a God-for-us. Thus the creed contains not so much information about God in case God needs our vote, but more so information about ourselves and our relationship to the God all about us, upon whose vote we all have been elected. No better commentary on the creedal affirmation of God can be found than the words of St. Paul: "Yet for us there is one God, the Father, from whom are all things and for whom we exist, and one Lord Jesus Christ, through whom are all things and through whom we exist" (1 Cor. 8:6).

Summary of Part Two of the Apostles' Creed

The six articles of the creed that follow the second article each contribute a descriptive clause that constitutes the "history" of Jesus the Christ, who is Lord. The events of Jesus' ministry and his subsequent death in Israel are historical. The further events of Jesus' life transcend history. Their creedal symbolization reflects the transformed insights of theology, a particular theology that uses narrative to interpret these *gesta Christi,* or "deeds of Christ." Thus the events need not have happened precisely as symbolized, although what is symbolized happened. Narrative theology is interpretive. Like all theology, it is a particular understanding of the faith community's experience of God. Much like an historical novel, the narrative theology of the Gospels is based upon the genuine deeds of Jesus, but adds to them the construction and redaction of the theological storyteller. The Christological center section of the creed tells the heart of this Gospel story succinctly and with much the same kerygmatic purpose.

Seven of the twelve articles of the creed, or eleven of the twenty clauses, make up the Christological content of part two. Article two establishes Jesus as Lord, and the following six articles proclaim his (3) birth, (4) suffering and death, (5) descent, (6) resurrection, (7) ascent and session, (8) and final coming. This is the largest section of the creed, and lends evidence that the heart of the Christian creed is found in the confession of its faith in Jesus Christ. The *gesta Christi* are listed in their bare outline, much as the *gesta Dei* were recapitulated in many short creedal passages in the Old Testament. Compare the following account of the deeds of the God of Israel:

> Then we cried to the Lord the God of our fathers, and the Lord heard our voice, and saw our affliction, our toil, and our oppression; and the Lord brought us out of Egypt with a mighty hand and an outstretched arm, with great terror, with signs and wonders; and he brought us into his place and gave us this land, a land flowing with milk and honey. (Deut. 26:7–10)

The creedal distillation of the deeds of Christ can similarly be found in the New Testament scriptures. For example, compare part two of the creed with the following passage from the First Letter of Peter:

> For Christ also died for sins once for all, the righteous for the unrighteous, that he might bring us to God, being put to death in the flesh but made alive in the spirit; in which he went and preached to the spirits in prison, who formerly did not obey, when God's patience waited in the days of Noah . . . through the resurrection of Jesus Christ, who has gone into heaven and is at the right hand of God, with angels, authorities, and powers, subject to him. (3:18–22)

The Christological section of the creed contains a major reversal of fortune. Jesus is humbled; Jesus is then exalted. Jesus descends to the stable; and then he ascends to glory. Let us rehearse the story in more detail. In article three Jesus is born of the Spirit and the woman Mary; he is born powerless into a microcosmic world. In article four, Jesus is judged wrongly, suffers his sentence, is crucified, truly dies, and is buried in a new grave; he is steeped in the injustice of this world and the darkness of death. In article five, Jesus descends into the depths, down into hell, back into the "shades" of the past unto the very beginning. At the bottom of this descending "V" Jesus reaches the nadir of distance from God and begins the ascent of the other side of the valley of death. In article six, "On the third day he rose again." In article seven, Jesus ascends to the heights, up to the heavens, forward into the future to the very ending of history, when the Kingdom in its fullness will be presented to his Father. He sits at the right hand, where now he is not judged wrongly, but he judges all ages rightly. Jesus suffers no more and will never die again. In article eight he is enthroned as Lord and reigns over the living and the dead, to judge and to fulfill the entire creation, past, present, and to come. Jesus is fully exalted to the zenith in glory; the lowly manger of Bethlehem is revealed as the hidden throne of the universe. In short, the six articles that describe the fate of Jesus Christ have a twofold dimension. He *suffers* on earth; he *sits* in heaven. "Suffers" includes all of the human condition and death at the end; "sits" includes all of the divine condition and sovereignty over creation. Jesus is disclosed as sovereign Lord, almighty in the macrocosmic universe, the infinite One who always has and always will encompass the Many.

Another way of putting this same paschal mystery is found in the wording of articles five and seven. Jesus descends into hell; Jesus ascends into heaven. The reversal of fortune is dramatic and complete. Jesus of Nazareth is revealed as the Christ by his life and death, which death, overcome in resurrection, proclaims that he is the only Son of God, exalted as Lord of the universe. Such becomes the creedal description of the paschal mystery. If the scheme above is maintained, there is a parallel relationship between articles one and two, and articles seven and eight. In the ascension and session, Jesus sits at the right hand of the Father (7), who is the "Father almighty, creator of heaven and earth" (1). And in the final judgment of living and dead (8), Jesus is Lord of the universe just as he was acclaimed "the only Son, Our Lord" (2). Thus the ascension and the session is actually a return of the Son to the bosom of the Father and to the sovereignty of the universe, which the Son of God always enjoyed as Lord of creation from its beginning to its end and as "true God from true God."

Jesus enters the created world of the Many that cannot be God and yet cannot be without God. Succinctly the creed proclaims that he is born, he suffers, he dies. This is the human story. We undergo our life. We are born without consent; we suffer events; we must all come to die. Jesus is steeped in the mystery of the Many that suffers from the seeming absence of God. In the return to his Father, in the resurrection, the ascension, and the sitting at the right hand, Jesus reenters the mystery of the One, the One infinite and sovereign God without whom the Many cannot be. Given creation as an impossible mystery that nonetheless has happened, if one asks how is the One God Lord of the Many, the answer is Jesus Christ our Lord, who was born, suffered, and so forth. Jesus was so intensely *from God* and into the world of the Many; he so intensely was born, suffered, and died. Furthermore, Jesus was so intensely *to God*, and Jesus was so fully back to God by his death, resurrection, and ascension to glory that he entered the world of the One completely. So all-embracing from the One into the Many, and so deliberately from the Many and back into the One was Jesus, that it dawned to the insight of faith that Jesus could only be Lord. So fulsome was Jesus' relationship to God that he had to be God. None other but the Lord could be so whole-heartedly from God and into this world, and return out of this world and be all given back to God. "Jesus is Lord" reveals the fullness of the mystery of the One and the Many.

In short, "Jesus is Lord" sums up the second part of the creed. We had already seen in article one how God was infinite and sovereign. Article two proclaims that the sovereignty of God extends to the Many of creation. God is Lord even of what is not God and yet cannot be away from God. In article three Jesus who is Lord proves sovereign over nature and is born of the Virgin Mary. In his passion and death he is sovereign over weakness and dying, over the night and the depth. Jesus is Lord of emptiness as well as Lord of fullness. In the resurrection of Jesus, he is Lord over life and death. In the ascension the Lordship of Jesus over the heavens as well as the earth, the future as well as the past, is celebrated. Part two of the creed is thus the celebration of the Lordship of Jesus, who is infinite and sovereign Lord, One and yet Many.

Summary of Part Three of the Apostles' Creed

Just as part two validates and confirms the promise of God as Father in part one of the creed, so part three reaffirms the promise of Jesus Christ as God with us. The Spirit continues the work of Jesus and consummates it. The Spirit in the church gives birth to Christians much as the Spirit in Mary gave birth to Jesus. Mary is now a symbol of the church. The assembly of holy church calls a separated humanity into a community of brothers and sisters of the one Lord Jesus. Now we might love each other as brother and sister of the one Father. The Spirit forgives sins, bringing harmonious life out of discordant death, just as Jesus rose from the dead, and the Father created from nothing. No greater culmination of God's deeds can be imagined than to reconcile sinners, to inspire love among enemies, to convert hard hearts, to create anew, now not out of neutral nothingness, but even out of hostile fear and suspicion.

The third part of the creed echoes the second and Christological part. The *gesta Christi* (deeds of Christ) were told in the form of narrative theology much like the Gospels. The *gesta Spiriti* (deeds of the Spirit), however, are told in the form of a more systematic theology like the Pauline epistles. Yet both parts of the creed talk about the Christ-event. The one account tells of the historical Christ, and the other tells of the historical church as the continuation of the life and work of Christ. Now are the "church times"; now are the "between times," between the coming of Jesus in Bethlehem and his final coming in glory. The incarnation will only be fulfilled completely in the parousia when the Lord comes to judge the living and the dead. Hence, part two of the creed is truly central, not only in position, but also in importance. The meaning of the first part of the creed, which extols God as Father, can only be understood fully in the revelation of the Son, and the true meaning of the church as the body of Christ can only be understood in the descent of the Holy Spirit. Christ is the face of the Father made known to us as the God of love, and Christ is the giver of the Spirit, known by us as the love of God dwelling in our hearts.

Throughout the creed, later articles assume earlier ones and build upon them. Because of the gift of the Holy Spirit, the Church is convoked by that same Spirit. Because of the assembly of people at the invitation of the Spirit, a holy people shares in the communion of saints and the common union of holy things that is sacramental life. Because of this shared life, the disunity of sin is forgiven and overcome. Because of this new communion with creation and the human community, the body will live in the resurrection of the flesh unto life everlasting. In other words, if the Spirit touches our heart and we think more of "we" (church) than of "me," then our sins, manifest in alienation, separation, isolation, loneliness, uncooperation, and hardheartedness, will be taken away in the forgiveness of sins. If your sins are forgiven, if you think of others before yourself, then you will not reap the wages of sin which is death, which death is me having only me. Rather you will reap the wages of life, of we, of church, of a reconciled community, which is life. Born of the Spirit's invitation, such a community will live, and its relationships will perdure. That spirit-filled life leads to the resurrection of the body and to that life which will never end.

One could make a case for the triumph of the Holy Spirit as the climax of the entire creed, and of part three in particular. Accordingly, the Spirit hovered over the waters of chaos in the beginning and gave existence and life to all creation. That same Spirit overshadowed Mary and gave birth to Jesus who is Lord. And that identical Spirit descends upon humankind gathered still today in the Pentecost upper room in expectation. Humanity in faith becomes baptized by fire and the Spirit. The holy church becomes temple of the Holy Spirit. To God the Father is appropriated the work of creation (part one), and to Jesus Christ his only Son belongs the incarnation of the Word made flesh (part two). To God the Holy Spirit is appropriated the work of sanctification in the world community that is the church throughout history (part three). It is entirely fitting that the creed be sung at the Eucharistic liturgy, whether in the simple elegance of chant or in the four-part splendor of Bach and Mozart. In the epiclesis of the Holy Mass, that same Spirit of God is called down upon the bread and wine, the expectant world of creation and human endeavor, so that all this may become by the power of the Spirit the living body of Christ. God is the giver, the gift, and the reception; God is Father, Son, and Holy Spirit. It is in that mystery of the approach of the infinite and triune God, the One in union with the Many, that inspired the creed in the first place, and which is daily celebrated and renewed in the liturgical prayer and joy of the Christian faithful.

APPENDIX

VERSIONS OF THE CREED

APOSTLES' CREED

parentheses = late-established additions

1   Credo in Deum
Patrem Omnipotentem
(Creatorem coeli et terrae)

2   Et in Jesum Christum
Filium ejus unicum
Dominum nostrum

3   Qui (conceptus) est de Spiritu Sancto
Natus ex Maria Virgine

4   (Passus) sub Pontio Pilato, crucifixus
(Mortuos) et sepultus

5   (Descendit ad inferna) [not in Nicene]

6   Tertia die resurrexit a mortuis

7   Ascendit ad coelos
Sedet ad dexteram (Dei) Patris (omnipotentis)

8   Inde venturus est
Judicare vivos et mortuos

9   Credo in Spiritum Sanctum

10   Sanctam Ecclesiam (Catholicam)

11   (Sanctorum Communionem) [not in Nicene]
Remissionem peccatorum

12   Carnis resurrectionem,
(Et vitam aeternam).

This creed identifies the late-established additions to the Apostles' Creed. The text is based on Heurtley's *Harmonia Symbolica*, pp. 118–120. In my arrangement "the descent," "the communion of saints," and the "resurrection of the body" differ in their position from that of Heurtley. I also include the "et" before "vitam aeternam." Neither Heurtley nor Denzinger (no. 30), which gives the standardized text from the *Breviarium Romanum* include this conjunction. Along with J. N. D. Kelly, I take the "et" from the *Ordo Romanus Antiquus*.

169

ICET TRANSLATION

1. I believe in God, the Father almighty,
2.   creator of heaven and earth.

3. I believe in Jesus Christ, his only Son, our Lord.
4.   He was conceived by the power of the Holy Spirit
5.   and born of the Virgin Mary.
6. He suffered under Pontius Pilate,
7.   was crucified, died, and was buried.
8. He descended to the dead.
9. On the third day he rose again.
10. He ascended into heaven,
11.   and is seated at the right hand of the Father.
12. He will come again to judge the living and the dead.

13. I believe in the Holy Spirit,
14.   the holy catholic Church,
15.   the communion of saints,
16.   the forgiveness of sins,
17.   the resurrection of the body,
18.   and the life everlasting. Amen.

The ICET version of the Apostles' Creed (International Consultation on English Texts). *Prayers We Have in Common*, 2d rev. ed. (Philadelphia: Fortress Press, 1975). The ICEL version of the Apostles' Creed (International Commission on English in the Liturgy) is identical.

TRANSLATION OF THE APOSTLES' CREED

1 I believe in God the Father all-powerful (all-sovereign)
   creator of heaven and earth

2 And in Jesus Christ
   his only son (one and only son)
   our Lord

3 Who was conceived by the Holy Spirit
   born of the virgin Mary

4 Suffered under Pontius Pilate
   was crucified
   was dead
   and was buried

5 He descended into hell (to the dead)

6 On the third day he rose (again) from the dead

7 He ascended into heaven
   is seated at the right hand of God the Father all-powerful (all-sovereign)

8 From where he will come to judge the living (quick) and the dead

9 I believe in the Holy Spirit (Ghost)

10 The holy catholic church

11 The communion of saints
   the forgiveness of sins

12 The resurrection of the body (the flesh)
   and life eternal (everlasting)

My translation of the Latin, done in a more literal fashion. See Novak's *Confessions of a Catholic*, pp. 20–24. Novak conveniently gathers for easy comparison the English translations by Liturgical Press, Benziger Bros., and Helicon Press. His discussion of the English in the Sunday missalettes raises the question of adequate translation.

TRANSLATION OF THE APOSTLES' CREED

1   I believe in God the Father all-sovereign
       creator of heaven and earth

2   And in Jesus Christ
       his one and only son
       our Lord

3   Who was conceived by the Holy Spirit
       born to the virgin Mary

4   Suffered under Pontius Pilate
       was crucified
       was dead
       and was buried

5   He descended into the underworld

6   On the third day he rose from the dead

7   He ascended into heaven
       is seated at the right hand of God the Father all-sovereign

8   From where he will come to judge the living and the dead

9   I believe in the Holy Spirit

10   The holy catholic church

11   The communion of saints
       the forgiveness of sins

12   The resurrection of the body
       and life eternal

My translation of the Latin, done in a more free fashion.

NICENO-CONSTANTINOPOLITAN CREED

italics = not in Apostles' Creed

Credo in *unum* Deum
Patrem Omnipotentem (pantocrator)
Factorem coeli et terrae
visibilium omnium et invisibilium

Et in *unum* Dominum Jesum Christum
Filium *Dei unigenitum*
Qui ex Patre natum ante omnia saecula.
(Deum de Deo,) [not in the Greek] *lumen de lumine, Deum verum de Deo vero,*
Genitum, non factum, consubstantialem (homoousion) *Patri*
per quem omnia facta sunt.

Qui propter nos homines et propter nostram salutem
descendit de coelis
Et incarnatus est de Spiritu Sancto
ex Maria Virgine, *et homo factus est.*

Crucifixus etiam *pro nobis* sub Pontio Pilato
Passus et sepultus est

Et resurrexit tertia die, *secundum Scripturas*

Et ascendit in coelum, sedet ad dexteram Patris

Et iterum venturus est *cum gloria*
judicare vivos et mortuous
cujus regni non erit finis

Et in Spiritum Sanctum *Dominum et vivificantem*
qui ex Patre (Filioque) [not in the Greek] *procedit*
Qui cum Patre et Filio simul adoratur et conglorificatur
qui locutus est per prophetas

Et *unam,* sanctam, catholicam, et *apostolicam* Ecclesiam

Confiteor unum baptisma in remissionem peccatorum

Et expecto resurrectionem *mortuorum*

Et vitam *venturi saeculi.* Amen

The Latin of the Niceno-Constantinopolitan Creed was taken from Denzinger, no. 150, p. 67. Denzinger took it from the official standardized Latin text in the *Missale Romanum.*

173

ICET TRANSLATION

1. We believe in one God,
2.   the Father, the Almighty,
3.   maker of heaven and earth,
4.   of all that is, seen and unseen.
5. We believe in one Lord, Jesus Christ,
6.   the only Son of God,
7.   eternally begotten of the Father,
8.   God from God, Light from Light,
9.   true God from true God,
10.   begotten, not made,
11.   of one Being with the Father.
12.   Through him all things were made.
13. For us men and for our salvation
14.   he came down from heaven:
15. by the power of the Holy Spirit
16.   he became incarnate from the Virgin Mary and was made man.
17. For our sake he was crucified under Pontius Pilate;
18.   he suffered death and was buried.
19.   On the third day he rose again
20.   in accordance with the Scriptures;
21.   he ascended into heaven
22.   and is seated at the right hand of the Father.
23. He will come again in glory to judge the living and the dead,
24.   and his kingdom will have no end.
25. We believe in the Holy Spirit, the Lord, the giver of life,
26.   who proceeds from the Father [and the Son].
27.   With the Father and the Son he is worshiped and glorified.
28.   He has spoken through the Prophets.
29.   We believe in one holy catholic and apostolic Church.
30.   We acknowledge one baptism for the forgiveness of sins.
31.   We look for the resurrection of the dead,
32.   and the life of the world to come. Amen.

ICET version of the Niceno-Constantinopolitan Creed. *Prayers We Have in Common* (Philadelphia: Fortress Press, 1975).

ICEL TRANSLATION

We believe in one God,
    the Father, the Almighty,
    maker of heaven and earth,
    of all that is seen and unseen.

We believe in one Lord, Jesus Christ,
    the only Son of God,
    eternally begotten of the Father,
    God from God, Light from Light,
    true God from true God,
    begotten, not made, one in Being with the Father.
    Through him all things were made.
    For us men and for our salvation
        he came down from heaven:
        by the power of the Holy Spirit
        he was born of the Virgin Mary, and became man.

For our sake he was crucified under Pontius Pilate;
    he suffered, died, and was buried.
    On the third day he rose again
        in fulfillment of the Scriptures;
    he ascended into heaven
        and is seated at the right hand of the Father.
He will come again in glory to judge the living and the dead,
    and his kingdom will have no end.

We believe in the Holy Spirit, the Lord, the giver of life,
    who proceeds from the Father and the Son.
    With the Father and the Son he is worshiped and glorified.
    He has spoken through the Prophets.
    We believe in one holy catholic and apostolic Church.
    We acknowledge one baptism for the forgiveness of sins.
    We look for the resurrection of the dead,
        and the life of the world to come. Amen.

ICEL version of the Niceno-Constantinopolitan Creed. *Vatican II Sunday Missal* (Boston: Daughters of St. Paul, 1974), pp. 596–597.

NICENO-CONSTANTINOPOLITAN CREED

italics = not in Apostles' Creed

I believe in *one* God
Father all-mighty (pantocrator)
Maker of heaven and earth,
   of all things visible and invisible.

And in *one* Lord Jesus Christ
His only Son
Who was born from the Father before all ages
(God from God) [not in the Greek] *light from light, true God from true God,*
Begotten, not made, one in substance (homoousion) *with the Father*
through whom everything is made.

Who on account of us human beings and because of our salvation
Came down from heaven
And was made flesh by the Holy Spirit from the Virgin Mary,
and was made man.

And He was crucified *for us* under Pontius Pilate
Suffered and was buried

The third day He rose up, *according to the Scriptures*

He ascended into heaven,
   and is seated at the right hand of the Father

From where he will come again *with glory*
to judge the living and the dead,
whose reign will never end.

And in the Holy Spirit *Lord and life-giver*
who from the Father (and the Son) [Filioque not in the Greek] *proceeds*
who with the Father and the Son is likewise adored and glorified
who has spoken through the prophets

And *one,* holy, catholic, and *apostolic* Church.

I confess one baptism for the forgiveness of sins.

And I await the resurrection of the *dead*

And the life *of the world to come.* Amen

My translation.

176

ENGLAND: CIRCA A.D. 1125

Old English, Old French, and Latin

Ic gelefe on Gode Faedera aelwealdend
Ieo crei en Deu le Perre tut puant
Credo in Deum Patrem Omnipotentem

1

Sceppend heofones and eorthan;
Le criatur de ciel e de terre
Creatorem coeli et terrae

— —

And on Helende Crist, Suna his anlich,
E en Jesu Crist, sun Fil uniel,
Et in Jesum Christum Filium ejus unicum

2

Drihten ure
Nostre Seinur
Dominum nostrum

— —

Syo the akynned is of tham Halig Gaste
Ki concevz est del Seint Esprit
Qui conceptus est de Spiritu Sancto

3

Boran of Marian tham maeden
Nez de Marie la [?]
Natus ex Maria Virgine

— —

Gethrowode under tham Pontiscam Pilate, and on rode ahangen
[?] ntien Pilate, crucifiez
Passus sub Pontio Pilato, crucifixus

4

Dead, and beberiged
Morz, e seveliz
Mortuus, et sepultus

— —

He adun astaeh to hellae;
Descedied as enfers
Descendit ad inferna

5

177

Thriddan degge he aras fram deatha
Et tierz jurn relevad de morz
Tertia die resurrexit a mortuis
— —

He astah to heofone
Muntad as ciels
Ascendit ad coelos
6

Sit on switran healfe Godes Faederes ealmihtig
Siet a la destre de Deu Perre tres tut puant
Sedet ad dexteram Dei Patris omnipotentis
— —

Thanen he is to cumene, and to demenna quicke and deade
7   Diluc est avenir jugier les vis e les morz
Inde venturus judicare vivos et mortuos
— —

Ic gelefe on Halig Gast
8   Jeo crei el Seint Espirit
Credo in Spiritum Sanctum
— —

And on halig gesomnunge fulfremede
9   Seinte Eglise Catholica
Sanctam Ecclesiam Catholicam
— —

Halegan hiniennesse
La communion des seintes choses
Sanctorum communionem
10

Forgyfenysse synna
Remissium des pecchiez
Remissionem peccatorum
— —

Flesces up arisnesse
11   Resurrectiun de charn
Carnis resurrectionem
— —

Lif eche	Beo hit swa
12 Vie pardurable	Seit feit
Vitam aeternam	Amen

From Charles Heurtley, *Harmonia Symbolica: A Collection of Creeds* (Oxford: Oxford University Press, 1858), pp. 92–93. This creed is interesting for its early and uninhibited translations from the Latin.

ENGLAND A.D. 1543

I beleve in God the Father almighty,
Maker of heaven and earth;

And in Jesu Christe, his onely Sonne,
Our Lorde;

Whiche was conceived by the Holy Goste, Borne of the Virgine Mary;

Suffred under Ponce Pylate, was crucified,
Dead, buried,
And descended into Hell;

And the third day he rose agein from deth;

He ascended into heaven;
And sitteth on the right hand of God the Father almighty;

From thens he shall come to judge the quicke and the deade,

I beleve in the Holy Goste;

The holy Catholike Churche;

The communyon of sayntes;
The forgyveness of synnes;

The resurrection of the body;

And the lyfe everlastynge. Amen.

A post-Reformation English creed. From Heurtley, *Harmonia Symbolica*, p. 100.

OLD ENGLISH METRICAL VERSION OF APOSTLES' CREED

I trow in God, fader of might,
    That alle has wroght,
Heven and erthe, day and night,
    And alle of noght.
And in Ihesu that God's Son is
    Al-onely,
Bothe God and mon, Lord endles,
    In him trow I;
Thurgh mekenes of tho holy gast,
    That was so milde,
He lyght in Mary mayden chast,
    Be-come a childe;
Under pounce pilat pyned he was,
    Us forto save,
Done on cros and deed he was,
    Layde in his grave;
The soul of him went into helle,
    Tho sothe to say;
Up he rose in flesshe and felle
    Tho tyryd day;
He stegh till heven with woundis wide,
    Thurgh his pouste;
Now sittes opon his fader right syde,
    In mageste;
Thethin shal he come us alle to deme
    In his manhede,
Qwyk and ded, alle that has ben
    In Adam sede,
Wel I trow in tho holi gost,
    And holi kirc that is so gode;

This metrical elaboration comes from Edgar Gibson's *The Three Creeds* (London: Longmans, Green, 1908), pp. 110–111. It is included here for the delight of the reader.

And so I trow that housel es
 Bothe flesshe and blode;
Of my synnes, forgyfnes,
 If I wil mende;
Up-risyng als-so of my flesshe,
 And lyf with-outen ende.

NOTES

Introduction

1. J. N. D. Kelly, *Early Christian Creeds*, 3d ed. (New York: David McKay Co., 1972). If you can read only one work on the history of the creed, this is the book.

2. See the bibliography at the end of this book for fuller citations.

3. J. P. Migne, *Patrologiae Cursus Completus*, Series Latina (Paris, 1844–64). Hereinafter referred to as *PL*. "Commentary on the Apostles' Creed": "Symbolum enim Graece et indicium dici potest, et collatio, hoc est quod plures in unum conferunt." *PL* 21:337.

4. "Explanatio Symboli ad Initiandos": "Symbolum Graece dicitur, Latine autem collatio." *PL* 17:1155.

5. Sermon #212: "Symbolum autem nuncupatur a similitudine quadam, translato vocabulo; quia symbolum inter se faciunt mercatores, quo eorum societas pacto fidei teneatur." *PL* 38:1058.

6. *Ancient Christian Writers*, vol. 20, trans. J. N. D. Kelly (Westminster, Md.: Newman Press, 1955). See his translation and notes on Rufinus' *Commentary on the Apostles' Creed*, especially pp. 101–102. See also Kelly, *Early Christian Creeds*, pp. 52–61.

7. Kelly, *Early Christian Creeds*, p. 61.

8. Song 8:6.

9. "Explanatio Symboli ad Initiandos": "Nunc tempus est et dies ut symbolum tradamus; quod symbolum est spiritale signaculum, cordis nostri meditatio, et quasi semper praesens custodia, certe thesaurus pectoris nostri." *PL* 17:1155.

10. "Haec est fides quae paucis verbis tenenda in Symbolo novellis christianis datur. Quae pauca verba fidelibus nota sunt, ut credendo subjugentur Deo, subjugati recte vivant, recte vivendo cor mundeat, corde mundato quod credunt intelligant." *PL* 40:196.

11. *The Christian Faith: An Essay on the Structure of the Apostles' Creed*, trans. Richard Arnandez (San Francisco: Ignatius Press, 1986), p. 9.

12. See the joint publication of the U.S.A. National Committee of the Lutheran World Federation and the Bishops' Commission for Ecumenical Affairs, *The Status of the Nicene Creed as Dogma of the Church*, ed. Paul C. Empie (Washington, D.C.: NCWC, 1965).

A Brief History of the Creed

1. "Explanatio Symboli ad Initiandos": "Sancti ergo apostoli in unum convenientes, breviarum fidei fecerunt, ut breviter fidei totius seriem comprehendamus." *PL* 17:1155.
2. "De Symbolo," in *The Fathers of the Church*, vol. 7, trans. Gerald G. Walsh (New York: Fathers of the Church, Inc., 1949), p. 53.
3. Henricus Denzinger, *Enchiridion Symbolorum*, 32d ed. (Rome: Herder, 1963). See the following references: Marcellus of Ancyra, No. 11; Rufinus of Aquileia, No. 16; and Nicetas of Remesiana, No. 19.
4. *Early Christian Creeds*, p. 166.
5. "De Singulis Libris Canonicis Scarapsus," Denzinger, *Enchiridion Symbolorum*, No. 28 and *PL* 89:1029.
6. In notes by J. N. D. Kelly to the translation of Rufinus of Aquileia's "Commentary on the Apostles' Creed" in *Ancient Christian Writers*, p. 16.
7. "De Symbolo": "Ista verba quae audistis, per divinas Scripturas sparsa sunt; sed inde collecta et ad unum redacta, ne tardorum hominum memoria laboraret; ut omnis homo possit dicere, possit tenere quod credit." *PL* 40:627.
8. John Courtney Murray's *The Problem of God* (New Haven, Conn.: Yale University Press, 1964) gives a succinct account of the debate about the interpolation of *homoousion* in the creed.
9. "Symbolum fidei, quo sancta Romana Ecclesia utitur, tamquam principium illud, in quo omnes, qui fidem Christi profitentur, necessario conveniunt, ac fundamentum firmum et unicum, contra quod portae inferi numquam praevalebunt, totidem verbis, quibus in omnibus ecclesiis legitur, experimendum esse censuit." Denzinger, *Enchiridion Symbolorum*, No. 1500.
10. *PL* 39:2189–90.

Article One

1. John Henry Newman, *A Grammar of Assent* (New York: The Catholic Publication Society, 1870), chapter 4, especially pp. 86–93.
2. Thomas Aquinas, *Collationes Credo in Deum*. In the Vivès edition (Paris, 1875), this work is entitled *In Symbolum Apostolorum scilicet "Credo in Deum" Expositio*, Vol. 27, Opusculum 7. In this work I am using my own translation of the unpublished but completed Leonine edition of these Lenten sermons-conferences (collationes) of Aquinas. See Aquinas's commentary in Part I on "I believe in God" in *The Sermon-Conferences of St. Thomas Aquinas on the Apostles' Creed* (Notre Dame, Ind.: University of Notre Dame Press, 1988).
3. All quotations from the Old Testament are taken from the Revised Standard Version, *The New Oxford Annotated Bible* (New York: Oxford University Press, 1973). New Testament quotations are taken from the *New American Bible*, rev. ed. with inclusive language (New York: Catholic Book Publishing Co., 1986).

4. See the *Oxford English Dictionary* under the word "believe." See also Wilfred Cantwell Smith, *Faith and Belief* (Princeton, N.J.: Princeton University Press, 1979), p. 76 and pp. 105–113. I discovered Smith after my own linguistic investigation, and our results are independently arrived at. I think he gives more credence to the "cor dare" derivation than I found warrant for.

5. Charles A. Heurtley, *Harmonia Symbolica: A Collection of Creeds* (Oxford: Oxford University Press, 1858), p. 94. Throughout my work I am indebted to insights gathered from Heurtley's scholarship in this book.

6. Mary McDermott Shideler, *A Creed for a Christian Skeptic* (Grand Rapids, Mich.: Wm. B. Eerdmans, 1968), p. 100.

7. Gregory Vlastos, *The Religious Way* (New York: The Woman's Press, 1934), p. 9. Cited in Shideler above, p. 100.

8. "Ipsum esse subsistens" might be translated as "very being subsisting." The meaning is this: God is not a being or nature that has existence; God is existence. Being is not given to God; God gives being to every being. God is being.

9. Heurtley, *Harmonia Symbolica*, p. 91. This creed is reproduced in the Appendix.

10. David Baily Harned, *Creed and Personal Identity: The Meaning of the Apostles' Creed* (Philadelphia: Fortress Press, 1981), p. 31.

11. "*Lex orandi, lex credendi*" is an ancient summary phrase that might be translated, "the law of praying is the law of believing." It means that the formulation of one's prayer reveals the formulation of one's belief.

Article Two

1. This theme of the role of women can be found in many of Paul Claudel's plays, especially "Break of Noon," trans. Wallace Fowlie (Regnery: Chicago, 1960) and "The Satin Slipper," trans. John O'Connor (New Haven, Conn.: Yale University Press, 1931).

2. Soren Kierkegaard, *Training in Christianity*, trans. Walter Lowrie (New York: Oxford University Press, 1941), see Part II, "The Offense," pp. 79–144.

3. "Gesta Dei" might be translated the "deeds of God." The implication is that the deeds are wonderful to behold and to chronicle.

4. Joseph Ratzinger, *Introduction to Christianity*, trans. J. R. Foster (New York: Herder and Herder, 1970). See "The Creed's Image of Christ," pp. 148–151.

5. See Michael Novak, *Confession of a Catholic* (San Francisco: Harper and Row, 1983), pp. 20–24. Novak conveniently gathers for easy comparison the English translations by Liturgical Press, Benziger Bros., and Helicon Press.

6. Arius was a priest and theologian of Alexandria. For the historical data surrounding the Nicene controversey, the classic source is J. N. D. Kelly's *Early Christian Creeds*. See also John Courtney Murray, *The Problem of God*.

7. Athanasius died in 373, but for many decades he was an outstand-
ing champion of the Nicene theology. The Arian theological issue was con-
founded with ecclesial political struggles, and Athanasius found himself
exiled several times.

8. "The Dedication Creed" in *Documents of the Christian Church*,
ed. Henry Bettenson, 2d ed. (New York: Oxford University Press, 1963), p. 41.

9. Murray, *Problem of God*, gives a succinct study of this development.

10. See under "Yahweh," *New Catholic Encyclopedia*, 14 (New York:
McGraw-Hill, 1967), pp. 1065–66.

11. For much of this discussion of the irrevocable bond of the incarnation I am indebted to Karl Rahner's masterful book, *Foundations of Christian Faith: An Introduction to the Idea of Christianity*, trans. William V. Dych
(New York: Seabury, 1978).

Article Three

1. The human egg was discovered only as recently as the early nine-
teenth century.

2. In Greek mythology Helen of Troy, whose beauty was legendary,
was born of a human mother, Leda, who was impregnated by Zeus, who ap-
proached her in the form of a swan.

3. See Aquinas, "Collationes Credo in Deum," at the end of the second article (Part IV). I give my own translation from the yet unpublished
Leonine edition: "(1) she [Mary] heard [the Word], 'the Holy Spirit will over-
shadow' and so forth [Luke 1:35]; (2) she consented through faith, 'Behold the
handmaid of the Lord' and so forth [Luke 1:38]; (3) she kept the word and carried it in her womb; (4) she brought the word forth, 'she brought forth her
first-born son' [Luke 2:7]; (5) she nourished the word and nursed it, whence
'Only a Virgin nursed' and so forth," (*Sermon Conferences of St. Thomas Aquinas*, p. 53). Thus the Christian in accepting faith by hearing repeats the mystery of the Word made flesh in Mary, the mother of God.

4. Gerard Manley Hopkins, *Poems and Prose of Gerard Manley Hopkins* (Harmondsworth, Middlesex: Penquin, 1953), p. 54.

5. Raymond E. Brown, *The Virginal Conception and Bodily Resurrection of Jesus* (New York: Paulist, 1973), pp. 21–96.

6. The Latin "propter nos homines" is often rendered "for us men." I
translated it "for us human beings." The word *homines* in Latin clearly means
men and women. The English word "homicide" reflects this generic status.
We have no such generic word in English for men and women. "Man" is often
employed for that purpose, but not without ambiguity. When the Nicene
Creed concludes the third article, "et *homo* factus est," it uses the same word
for "human being." Latin uses a different word *vir* (virile) for a male human
being. The humanity of Jesus and the humanity of men and women, and
not their sexual difference, seems to be the specific intent in the choice of
words in the creed.

7. St. Athanasius, *On the Incarnation*, trans. Penelope Lawson (New York: Macmillan, 1946).

Article Four

1. "Ecce homo" is usually translated, "behold the man." See the discussion of the Latin word *homo* in note 6 of article three.

2. See Sophocles' dramatic *Oedipus* trilogy.

3. Georg Wilhelm Friedrich Hegel, *Philosophy of History*, trans. J. Sibree (New York: Dover, 1956), p. 21.

4. "Homo lupus homini" might be translated "humanity, a wolf to humanity."

5. For this analysis I am indebted to lectures by Raymond E. Brown.

6. Athanasius, *On the Incarnation*, chapter 4, "The Death of Christ," pp. 31–40.

7. Sebastian Moore, *The Crucified Jesus is No Stranger* (Minneapolis: Seabury, 1977).

8. See Ernst Becker, *The Denial of Death* (New York: Free Press, 1973). This book influenced Moore's writings, above.

9. See Reginald H. Fuller, *The Formation of the Resurrection Narratives* (Philadelphia: Fortress Press, 1980), p. 15.

Article Five

1. Raymond Nogar's *Lord of the Absurd* (New York: Herder and Herder, 1966) inspired my choice of words.

2. Hans Kung, *Eternal Life?* trans. Edward Quinn (New York: Doubleday, 1984), pp. 125–126.

3. Other passages from scripture are sometimes considered as the foundation for the doctrine of the descent into hell: thus, Jonah 2:4–7, Mt. 12:40, Mt. 27:52, John 5:25, Acts 2:27–31, Rom. 10:6–7, Eph. 4:9–10, Heb. 2:14–15, and Rev. 1:17–18.

4. See Kelly, *Early Christian Creeds*, p. 290.

5. See "A Commentary on the Apostles' Creed," in vol. 20, *Ancient Christian Writers*, pp. 52 and 62. Kelly's introduction is very helpful in giving an historical overview.

6. "De Singulis Libris Canonicis Scarapsus." *PL* 89:1034.

7. Homer, *The Odyssey*, Book XI.

8. See "Gehenna" in *Harper's Bible Dictionary* (San Franciso: Harper and Row, 1985).

9. Dante Alighieri, *The Divine Comedy*. See Canto XXXIV of "The Inferno."

10. Taken from the record of Joan of Arc's trial in Regine Pernoud, *Joan of Arc* (New York: Stein and Day, 1966), p. 183.

11. See Jacques Le Goff, *The Birth of Purgatory,* trans. Arthur Gold-hammer (Chicago: University of Chicago Press, 1984).

12. *Catholicism,* one-volume ed. (Minneapolis: Winston, 1981), p. 1151.

Article Six

1. Brown, *Virginal Conception,* pp. 69–130. See also Reginald Fuller, *The Formation of the Resurrection Narratives* (Philadelphia: Fortress, 1980), and Herman Hendrickx, *The Resurrection Narratives in the Synoptic Gospels* (London: Geoffrey Chapman, 1984).

2. Athanasius, *On the Incarnation,* Paragraph 26, p. 41.

3. See the *Oxford English Dictionary* under the word "again."

4. For this overall theoretical consideration I again acknowledge my indebtedness to Raymond E. Brown.

Article Seven

1. Helmut Thielicke, *I Believe: The Christian's Creed,* trans. John W. Doberstein and H. George Anderson (Philadelphia: Fortress Press, 1968), p. 192.

2. Ibid.

Article Eight

1. C. S. Lewis, *Till We Have Faces* (New York: Harcourt, Brace, 1956).

2. John Milton, *Paradise Lost,* I:263, "Better to reign in Hell, than serve in Heav'n."

3. Dag Hammarskjold, *Markings,* trans. Leif Sjoberg and W. H. Auden (New York: Knopf, 1966), p. 205.

4. For this insight I am indebted to the lectures of the scripture scholar, Roland Murphy, O. Carm.

5. See Kelly, *Early Christian Creeds,* chapter 9, especially p. 338.

Article Nine

1. See the opening paragraph of Aquinas, "Collationes Credo in Deum," article ten (part 12), which is headed "the holy catholic church."

2. See Kelly, *Early Christian Creeds,* chapter 11, pp. 332–367.

3. Denzinger, *Enchiridion Symbolorum,* No. 11, p. 21.

4. Kelly, *Early Christian Creeds,* pp. 358–367.

5. See *New Catholic Encyclopedia,* vol. 5 (New York: McGraw-Hill, 1967), under "filoque," pp. 913–914.

6. Hopkins, *Poems*, p. 27.

7. *Missale Romanum* (Rome: Desclee, 1937), p. 340.

Article Ten

1. *Ancient Christian Writers*, vol. 20, p. 71.

2. Thielicke, *I Believe*, p. 233.

3. "Ex opere operato" might be translated "from the work being done."

4. Heurtley, *Harmonia Symbolica*, p. 97.

5. Karl Rahner, an address delivered April 8, 1979, printed in *Theological Studies* 40 (1979): 716–727.

6. See Vatican II, *Gaudium et Spes*, "The Church in the Modern World."

7. Albert Van Den Heuvel in *A New Look at the Apostles' Creed*, ed. Gerhard Rein, trans. David LeFort (Minneapolis: Augsburg, 1968), pp. 69–70.

Article Eleven

1. Kelly, *Early Christian Creeds*, p. 388.

2. Heurtley, *Harmonia Symbolica*, p. 93. This creed is reproduced in the Appendix.

3. Jan Milic Lochman, *The Faith We Confess*, trans. David Lewis (Philadelphia: Fortress Press, 1984), p. 211.

4. Leo Tolstoy, *War and Peace*, trans. Louise and Aylmer Maude (New York: Simon and Schuster, 1954), p. 1179.

Article Twelve

1. Andrew Marvell, "To His Coy Mistress," in *The Poems of Andrew Marvell*, ed. Hugh Macdonald (London: Routledge and Kegan Paul, 1952), p. 22.

2. Ladislaus Boros, *Living in Hope* (New York: Herder and Herder, 1971), p. 34.

3. E. J. Fortman, *Everlasting Life: Towards a Theology of the Future Life* (New York: Alba House, 1986), p. 295.

4. Paul Claudel, "Break of Noon" (Chicago: Regnery, 1960).

5. *My Bones Being Wiser* (Middletown, Conn.: Wesleyan University Press, 1963), p. 45.

6. See Aquinas, "Collationes Credo in Deum," part 14 on the "resurrection of the body."

7. See Fortman, *Everlasting Life*, p. 297.

8. Flannery O'Connor. See her short story, "The Displaced Person," in *The Complete Stories* (New York: Farrar, Straus and Giroux, 1971).

9. *Ordo Romanus Antiquus* is a tenth-century ceremonial book. Kelly,

(*Early Christian Creeds*, p. 369) uses it as his base for the *textus receptus*, and it does include the conjunction "and" before "life eternal." However, the *Breviarium Romanum*, which in the sixteenth century was edited by the Vatican in an attempt to standardize the creed for the purpose of communal prayer, does not include the conjunction. Insofar as there is an official ecclesial text, it should be considered the breviary text, although that text may be deficient in this particular regard.

10. Gerhard Ebeling, "And the Life Everlasting," in *A New Look at the Apostles' Creed*, ed. Gerhard Rein (Minneapolis: Augsburg, 1969), pp. 85–86.

11. Dylan Thomas, "Do not go gentle into that good night," in *Collected Poems* (London: J. M. Dent, 1952), p. 128.

Summary

1. *The Idea of a University*, reprint (Notre Dame, Ind.: University of Notre Dame Press, 1982), Discourse II, p. 27.

BIBLIOGRAPHY
OF BOOKS IN ENGLISH
Concerning the Apostles' Creed
and the Nicene Creed,
Written since 1850.

Titles which I have seen and found helpful I mark with an asterisk

*Armstrong, Claude Blakely. *Creeds and Credibility.* Oxford: Mowbray, 1969.

Backemeyer, Frederick W. *This Abiding Creed: An Unconventual Approach to the Apostles' Creed.* Grand Rapids, Mich.: Zondervan, 1940.

*Badcock, Francis John. *The History of the Creeds.* New York: Macmillan, 1930.

*Barclay, William. *The Apostles' Creed for Everyman.* New York: Harper and Row, 1967.

*Barr, O. Sydney. *From the Apostles' Faith to the Apostles' Creed.* New York: Oxford University Press, 1964.

*Barth, Karl. *Credo: A Presentation of the Chief Problems of Dogmatics with Reference to the Apostles' Creed.* Trans. J. Strathearn McNab. New York: Scribner, 1936.

*————. *Dogmatics in Outline.* Trans. G. T. Thomson. New York: Philosophical Library, 1949.

*Basset, Bernard. *And Would You Believe It! Thoughts about the Creed.* New York: Doubleday, 1976.

Beeching, H. C. *The Apostles' Creed.* New York: Dutton, 1905.

Bell, G. K. *The Meaning of the Creed.* New York: Macmillan, 1917.

Bethune-Baker, James F. *The Faith of the Apostles' Creed.* London: Macmillan, 1918.

*Bindley, T. Herbert. *The Ecumenical Documents of the Faith.* Westport, Conn.: Greenwood Press, 1980.

Blair, Harold Arthur. *A Creed before the Creeds.* New York: Longmans, 1955.

Briggs, Charles Augustus. *The Fundamental Christian Faith.* New York: Scribner, 1913.

————. *Theological Symbolics.* New York: Scribner, 1914.

*Brunner, Emil. *I Believe in the Living God.* Trans. John Holden. Philadelphia: Westminster, 1961.

Bryan, David B. *From Bible to Creed: A New Approach to the Sunday Creed.* Wilmington, Del.: Glazier, 1988.

*Burn, A. E. *An Introduction to the Creeds and to the Te Deum.* London: Methuen, 1899.

———. *Facsimiles of the Creeds from Early Manuscripts.* London: Harrison, 1909.

*———. *The Nicene Creed.* London: Rivingtons, 1913.

*———. *The Apostles' Creed.* London: Rivingtons, 1914.

*Burnaby, John. *The Belief of Christendom: A Commentary on the Nicene Creed.* London: S.P.C.K. (Society for Promoting Christian Knowledge), 1963.

Callow, C. *A History of the Origin and Development of the Creeds.* London: E. Stock, 1899.

Cassels, Louis. *What's the Difference?* New York: Doubleday, 1965.

*Claudel, Paul. *I Believe in God: A Meditation on the Apostles' Creed.* Ed. Agnes du Sarment. Trans. Helen Weaver. New York: Holt, Rinehart and Winston, 1963.

*Cullmann, Oscar. *The Earliest Christian Confessions.* London: Lutterworth, 1949.

Curtis, William. *A History of Creeds and Confessions of Faith in Christendom and Beyond.* New York: Scribner, 1912.

*Danker, Frederick W. *Creeds in the Bible.* St. Louis: Concordia, 1966.

Davies, John Dudley. *Creed and Conflict.* Guildford, Surrey: Lutterworth, 1979.

*Day, Gardiner Mumford. *The Apostles' Creed: An Interpretation for Today.* New York: Scribner, 1963.

Devine, Arthur. *The Creed Explained.* New York: Benziger, 1892.

Douglass, Earl L. *The Faith We Live By: An Exposition of the Apostles' Creed.* Nashville, Tenn.: Cokesbury, 1937.

Du Bose, Henry W. *We Believe: A Study of the Apostles' Creed.* Richmond, Va.: John Knox Press, 1960.

Empie, Paul, ed. *The Status of the Nicene Creed as Dogma of the Church.* Washington, D.C.: NCWC, 1965.

Engelder, Theodore. *Popular Symbolics.* St. Louis: Concordia, 1934.

Evans, Robert F. *Making Sense of the Creeds.* New York: Association Press, 1964.

*Evely, Louis. *Credo.* Trans. Rosemary Sheed. Notre Dame, Ind.: Fides, 1967.

*Forell, George. *Understanding the Nicene Creed.* Philadelphia: Fortress, 1965.

*Fuhrmann, Paul. *An Introduction to the Great Creeds of the Church.* Philadelphia: Westminster, 1960.

Geikie-Cobb, William. *Mysticism and the Creed.* London: Macmillan, 1914.

*German Catechetical Association. *Credo: A Catholic Catechism.* Trans. Sister Benedict Davies. London: Geoffrey Chapman, 1983.

Gerrish, Brian Albert. *The Faith of Christendom.* Cleveland: World Pub. Co., 1963.

Gibson, Edgar. *The Three Creeds.* London: Longmans, 1908.

*Gilles, Anthony E. *The People of the Creed*. Cincinnati: St. Anthony Messenger Press, 1986.

Goodwin, Harvey. *The Foundations of the Creed*. 3d ed. New York: Dutton, 1899.

Graf, Arthur. *The Apostles' Creed*. Waco, Texas: Faith Pub. Co., 1978.

Greg, William R. *The Creed of Christendom*. London: Chapman, 1851.

*Harnack, Adolf. *The Apostles' Creed*. London: A. & C. Black, 1901.

*Harned, David Bailey. *Creed and Personal Identity: The Meaning of the Apostles' Creed*. Philadelphia: Fortress, 1981.

Harrison, Charles George. *The Creed for the Twentieth Century*. London: Longmans, 1923.

Harvey, W. W. *The History and Theology of the Three Creeds*. 2 vols. Cambridge: J. Deighton, 1854.

Hedley, George. *The Symbol of the Faith: A Study of the Apostles' Creed*. New York: Macmillan, 1948.

*Hellwig, Monika. *The Christian Creeds: A Faith to Live By*. Dayton, Ohio: Pflaum, 1973.

Heurtley, Charles A. *Harmonia Symbolica: A Collection of Creeds*. Oxford: Oxford University Press, 1858.

———. *On Faith and the Creed*. 3d ed. London: Parker, 1889. See also *De Fide et Symbolo*. 4th ed. London: Parker, 1889.

———. *A History of the Earlier Formularies of Faith*. London: Parker, 1892.

Ileana, Princess. *Meditations on the Nicene Creed*. New York: Morehouse-Gorham, 1958.

Johnston, James Wesley. *The Creed and the Prayer*. New York: Eaton and Mains, 1896.

Joinville, Jean. *Text and Iconography for Joinville's Credo*. Cambridge, Mass.: Mediaeval Academy of America, 1958.

*Kelly, J. N. D. *Early Christian Creeds*. 3d ed. London: Longmans, 1972.

*Kemmer, Alfons. *The Creed in the Gospels*. Trans. Urban Schnaus. New York: Paulist, 1986.

Kevane, Eugene. *Creed and Catechetics*. Westminster, Md.: Christian Classics, 1978.

Klotsche, Ernest Heinrich. *Christian Symbolics*. Burlington, Iowa: Lutheran Literary Board, 1929.

*Knox, Ronald. *The Creed in Slow Motion*. New York: Sheed and Ward, 1949.

Kunze, Johannes. *The Apostles' Creed and the New Testament*. New York: Funk and Wagnalls, 1912.

Lamont, Daniel. *The Church and the Creeds*. London: J. Clarke, 1923.

Leighton, Robert. *Expositions on the Creed, the Lord's Prayer, and the Ten Commandments*. New York: R. Carter, 1858.

*Leith, John H. *Creeds of the Churches*. Richmond, Va.: John Knox Press, 1973.

*Lochman, Jan Milic. *The Faith We Confess: An Ecumenical Dogmatics*. Trans. David Lewis. Philadelphia: Fortress, 1984.

Lockerbie, D. Bruce. *The Apostles' Creed*. Wheaton, Ill.: Victor Books, 1977.

*Lubac, Henri de. *The Christian Faith: An Essay on the Structure of the Apostles' Creed*. Trans. Richard Arnandez. San Francisco: Ignatius Press, 1986.

Lumby, Joseph. *The History of the Creeds*. Cambridge: Deighton, Bell and Co., 1887.

*MacGregor, Geddes. *The Nicene Creed, Illumined by Modern Thought*. Grand Rapids, Mich.: W. B. Eerdmans, 1980.

Maclear, G. F. *An Introduction to the Creeds*. London: Macmillan, 1890.

Major, H. D. A. *The Church's Creeds and the Modern Man*. London: Skeffington, 1933.

Malden, R. H. *Christian Belief: A Short Exposition of the Apostles' Creed*. London: National Society, 1942.

*Marthaler, Berard L. *The Creed*. Mystic, Conn.: Twenty-Third Publications, 1986.

McDermott, Timothy. *Beyond Questions and Answers*. New York: Herder and Herder, 1968.

McFayden, Donald. *Understanding the Apostles' Creed*. New York: Macmillan, 1927.

McGiffert, Arthur Cushman. *The Apostles' Creed: Its Origin, its Purpose, and its Historical Interpretation*. New York: Scribner, 1902.

Mehl, Paul. *Classic Christian Creeds*. Boston: United Church Press, 1964.

Mohler, Johann Adam. *Symbolism*. London: Gibbings, 1906.

Moment, John J. *We Believe*. New York: Macmillan, 1942.

Montgomery, James Alan. *The Christian Creed and History*. Evanston, Ill.: Seabury-Western Theological Seminary, 1935.

Mortimer, Alfred G. *The Creeds*. London: Longmans, 1902.

Murray, John Courtney. *The Problem of God*. New Haven, Conn.: Yale University Press, 1964.

Neufeld, Vernon H. *The Earliest Christian Confessions*. Leiden: E. J. Brill, 1963.

Neve, Juergen Ludwig. *Churches and Sects of Christendom*. Burlington, Iowa: Lutheran Literary Board, 1940.

*Novak, Michael. *Confessions of a Catholic*. San Francisco: Harper and Row, 1983.

Palmer, Frederic. *Studies in Theologic Definition Underlying the Apostles' and Nicene Creeds*. New York: Dutton, 1895.

*Pannenberg, Wolfhart. *The Apostles' Creed in the Light of Today's Questions*. Trans. Margaret Kohl. Philadelphia: Westminster Press, 1972.

*Paul VI. "The Credo of the People of God." Boston: St. Paul Editions, 1968.

Pearson, John. *An Exposition on the Creed*. Oxford: Clarendon, 1890.

* *Prayers We Have in Common*. By the International Consultation on English Texts. 2d rev. ed. Philadelphia: Fortress, 1975.

Quick, Oliver Chase. *Doctrines of the Creed: Their Basis in Scripture and their Meaning Today*. London: Nisbet, 1938.

*Ratzinger, Joseph. *Introduction to Christianity.* Trans. J. R. Foster. New York: Herder and Herder, 1969.

*Rein, Gerhard, ed. *A New Look at the Apostles' Creed.* Minneapolis: Augsburg, 1969.

Rolfus, Hermann. *Illustrated Explanation of the Apostles' Creed.* New York: Benziger, 1901.

Routley, Erik. *Creeds and Confessions.* London: Duckworth, 1962.

Rushdoony, Rousas. *The Foundations of Social Order: Studies in the Creeds.* Nutley, N.J.: Presbyterian and Reformed Pub. Co., 1972.

*Schaff, Philip. *The Creeds of Christendom.* New York: Harper, 1877.

*Shideler, Mary McDermott. *A Creed for a Christian Skeptic.* Grand Rapids, Mich.: W. B. Eerdmans, 1968.

Skilton, John H., ed. *Scripture and Confession.* Nutley, N.J.: Presbyterian and Reformed Pub. Co., 1973.

Skrine, John. *Creed and the Creeds: Their Function in Religion.* New York: Longmans, 1911.

Sloan, Harold Paul. *The Apostles' Creed.* New York: Methodist Book Concern, 1930.

———. *Christian Choice in Basic Truth: An Interpretation of the Apostles' Creed.* Butler, Ind.: Highley, 1959.

Smart, James D. *The Creed in Christian Teaching.* Philadelphia: Westminster, 1962.

Smith, Dana Prom. *An Old Creed for a New Day.* Philadelphia: Fortress, 1975.

Smith, Harold. *The Creeds: Their History, Nature and Use.* New York: Fleming H. Revell, 1912.

Sneath, Elias Hershey. *Shall We Have a Creed?* New York: Century, 1925.

Stewart, Alexander. *Creeds and the Churches: Studies in Symbolics.* New York: Hodder and Stoughton, 1916.

Swainson, Charles. *The Nicene and Apostles' Creeds.* London: J. Murray, 1875.

Swanston, Hamish. *A Language for Madness: The Abuse and Use of Christian Creeds.* Assen: Van Gorcum, 1976.

Swete, Henry. *The Apostles' Creed: Its Relation to Primitive Christianity.* Cambridge: Cambridge University Press, 1899.

*Thielicke, Helmut. *I Believe: The Christian's Creed.* Trans. John Doberstein and H. George Anderson. Philadelphia: Fortress, 1968.

Timiadis, Emilianos. *The Nicene Creed.* Philadelphia: Fortress, 1983.

*Torrance, Thomas. *The Incarnation: Ecumenical Studies in the Nicene-Constantinopolitan Creed, A.D. 381.* Edinburgh: Handsel, 1981.

*Underhill, Evelyn. *The School of Charity: Meditation on the Christian Creed.* New York: David McKay, 1962.

Van Baalen, Jan K. *Our Christian Heritage: An Exposition of the Apostolic Creed, the Ten Commandments and the Lord's Prayer.* Grand Rapids, Mich.: W. B. Eerdmans, 1949.

Vogt, Von Ogden. *The Primacy of Worship.* Boston: Starr King Press, 1958.

Westcott, B. F. *The Historic Faith: Short Lectures on the Apostles' Creed.* London: Macmillan, 1883.

Wheeler, Henry. *The Apostles' Creed: An Examination of its History and an Exposition of its Contents.* New York: Eaton and Mains, 1912.

*Wingren, Gustaf. *Credo: The Christian View of Faith and Life.* Trans. Edgar Carlson. Minneapolis: Augsburg, 1981.